CITYSPOTS
STOC▮

Barbara Radcliffe▮
and Stillman Rogers

GW00363875

Written by Barbara Radcliffe Rogers and Stillman Rogers
Front cover photograph copyright Alamy Images

Produced by 183 Books
Design/layout/maps: Chris Lane and Lee Biggadike
Editorial/project management: Stephen York

Published by Thomas Cook Publishing
A division of Thomas Cook Tour Operations Limited
PO Box 227, Units 15/16, Coningsby Road
Peterborough PE3 8SB, United Kingdom
email: books@thomascook.com
www.thomascookpublishing.com
+44 (0) 1733 416477

First edition © 2006 Thomas Cook Publishing
Text © 2006 Thomas Cook Publishing
Other maps © 2006 Thomas Cook Publishing
ISBN-13: 978-1-84157-587-2
ISBN-10: 1-84157-587-9
Project Editor: Kelly Anne Pipes
Production/DTP: Steven Collins

Printed and bound in Spain by GraphyCems

CONTENTS

SYMBOLS & ABBREVIATIONS

The following symbols are used throughout this book:

- **☏** telephone
- **🖷** fax
- **🌐** website address
- **ⓐ** address
- **🕐** opening times
- **🚇** public transport connections

The following symbols are used on the maps:

- **ℹ** Tourist Information Office
- **✈** Airport

Hotels and restaurants are graded by approximate price as follows:
K budget price **KK** mid-range price **KKK** expensive

24-HOUR CLOCK

All times in this book are given in the 24-hour clock system used widely in Europe and in most international transport timetables.

▶ *Impressive buildings are reflected in the waters surrounding the city*

Introduction

Stockholm wraps its arms around the harbour, embracing a fleet of white ferries that slip continually in and out of its grasp. The sea and the city are inseparable. Nearly every cityscape is either reflected in or framed by water, and neighbourhoods are defined by the 14 islands on which they are built.

Getting from one place to another usually means crossing a bridge, but will also likely involve crossing a park. The former vegetable garden of the Royal palace, in the heart of the shopping district, is a park, and others appear at every turn. Only minutes from the centre, the island of Djurgarden is a vast park, studded here and there with museums and attractions, but essentially green. Locals are fond of pointing out that Stockholm is one third water, one third green belt and one third city.

The other thing that visitors notice is that Stockholm is an intensely Swedish city, more representative of the country as a whole than most capitals are. All but one-tenth of its 1.6 million inhabitants are Swedes, and although ethnic touches of other cultures appear in a restaurant or market here and there, no one would mistake any street for anywhere but Sweden. At every turn is another example of the Swedish design that people here value so intensely.

This is a very visual city, its buildings well kept, its streets clean, its parks and gardens manicured, its people well-dressed and its squares adorned with public art. It is also a very walkable city, easy to explore on foot, with its sights close together, its neighbourhoods well defined and plenty of cafés and park benches to break the journey. Because the city is so attractive, you will want to explore it on foot, enjoying the sudden surprises as a street opens suddenly onto the water, or the turn of a corner brings you into a square surrounded by elegant buildings and adorned with sculpture.

It would be a shame, however, to treat Stockholm as just another pretty face. There's far more to it than that, so be sure to allow time to meet the locals and to join in local activities. Jog along the water's edge in the morning, take a ferry to a small island, stop for coffee in cafés, sit on the grass for a free concert, step up to the bar in a neighbourhood pub. You'll soon find yourself part of the exciting milieu that is Stockholm.

🔺 *There are plenty of opportunities to find a souvenir of your stay*

When to go

Scandinavian summers are short, but intense, with long daylight hours lasting well into the night. You have a better chance of having a holiday filled with sunlit days if you travel in June and July. From June 24, the midsummer holiday, through late July is when most Swedes have holidays, so expect the archipelago to be crowded.

The season when attractions keep the longest hours, and when smaller ones are open daily, begins in early June and ends in mid-August. Many smaller attractions will add a few weeks of weekends-only opening spring and fall, remaining closed for the long winter.

Spring and fall are pleasant, with uncertain weather. Winter is long, lasting from November through March. Daylight hours are short then, but weather often tends to be clear and crisp. Snow may fall often, but it seldom lasts long on the ground because of the moderating effect of the sea. While many archipelago lodgings and restaurants close in the winter, a few are open. But be sure to book ahead, since boats are fewer and many places open only when they have guests arriving. Stockholm rocks on all winter, with the action moving inside to cosier surroundings.

ANNUAL EVENTS

Most offices, banks and shops – even restaurants – close for public holidays. Banks may also close the day before a holiday. A full calendar of month-by-month events is listed at www.stockholmtown.se.

January

New Year's Concert The Storkyrkan Chamber Orchestra and chorus perform Beethoven's Ninth Symphony at the Cathedral. ③ Trångsund 1. ① 08.723.3016. ⓦ www.sthdomkyrko.com. Tickets: ① 077.170.7070.

April

Walpurgis Night (30 April). A public holiday celebrated throughout Sweden with bonfires. Stockholm's is at the terrace on Riddarholmen, or in Skansen Park, where admission is charged.

May

May Day Public holiday, observed by low-key rallies and gatherings of left-leaning action groups.

Opera and ballet Opening of summer season of opera and ballet which runs through June. Royal Swedish Opera (Kungliga Operan) Box Office ☎ 08.24.8240. 🖷 08.791.4444. 🌐 www.operan.se

Stockholm Spectacle Gamla Stan in late May is the scene of 18th-century pageantry, dancing and parades, along with a craft market.

Restaurangernas Dag Restaurants set up booths in Kungstradgarden, selling samples of their specialties, a good way to try dishes from fine restaurants without having to buy a whole meal.

June

Parkteatern Free performances (through August) that range from circus to dance and music, held in public parks. ☎ 08.505.20284. 🌐 www.stadsteatern.stockholm.se

Music pa Slottet Evening concerts of classical, folk and jazz continue through August inside the Royal Palace. ☎ 08.10.8800. 🌐 www.royalfestivals.se

National Day Public Holiday, new in 2005, celebrated with an evening programme at Skansen, with bands, ceremony and entertainment attended by the Swedish Royal Family.

23–25 June Midsummer's Eve, Midsummer's Day Public holidays, celebrated throughout the country with cookouts, picnics and family gatherings (see page 12).

July
Stockholm Jazz Festival World-rated artists perform all kinds of jazz on Skeppsholmen. ☎ 08.556.14564. Ⓦ www.stockholmjazz.com

August
Stockholm Pride Scandinavia's largest gay festival;
Ⓦ www.stockholmpride.org.
Midnattsloppet Thousands of runners compete in a late-night race through Södermalm, a grand excuse for everyone else to party all night. ☎ 08.649.7171. Ⓦ www.midnattsloppet.com

September
Opera and ballet season opens at Royal Swedish Opera. Box Office: ☎ 08.24.8240. ☎ 08.791.4444. Ⓦ www.operan.se

🔺 *Celebrations for National Day – the newest public holiday in Sweden's calendar*

December

Christmas Markets Kungstradgarden, Skansen, Rosendals Palace and Stortorget all host holiday crafts markets.

31 Nyärsafton (New Year's Eve Celebration) The old year is rung out with live music and fireworks. Skansen Outdoor Museum, Djurgårdsslätten 49-51, Djurgården, ☎ 08.442.8000 (info 24 hours), 08.578.90005. Ⓦ www.skansen.se

PUBLIC HOLIDAYS

New Year's Day 1 Jan

Epiphany 6 Jan

Maundy Thursday late Mar/early Apr

Good Friday late Mar/early Apr

Easter Sunday late Mar/early Apr

Easter Monday late Mar/early Apr

Walpurgis Night 30 Apr

May Day 1 May

Ascension Day May

Whit Sunday May/June

National Day 6 June

Midsummer's Eve, Midsummer's Day 23–25 June

All Saints Day Nov

Christmas Eve 24 Dec

Christmas Day 25 Dec

Boxing Day 26 Dec

New Year's Eve 31 Dec

Midsommar

At the summer solstice, when the days are longest and nights shortest, Sweden celebrates Midsummer's Eve. The holiday is no longer precisely on the solstice, but has been set at the third Friday and Saturday of June, so families can enjoy the weekend together. It's an occasion to go to a country house or a cottage on the archipelago, or to simply take a picnic to the countryside or a park.

A maypole – *majstång* in Swedish – is at the centre of the most traditional celebrations, a tall pole decorated with garlands of leaves and flower. The decorated pole is raised and everyone sings or dances beneath it. Flower crowns are another tradition, woven of fresh flowers. Both of these customs arise in ancient pagan festivals celebrating the summer and hoping for abundant harvests, but today Midsummer's Eve is a good excuse for a day in the country and a good party.

The traditional foods are new potatoes with dill and pickled herring or smoked fish in infinite variety, accompanied by beer and schnapps, topped off by the season's first strawberries for dessert.

Although many Swedes celebrate at private gatherings of family and friends, there are plenty of public activities that visitors can join it. Any farm museum will have a celebration with a maypole and in Stockholm, Skansen celebrates for three days. Visitors help make the flower garlands that decorate the maypole, and can join in the dancing after it is raised. It's particularly colourful there because many people are in old traditional costumes. It's also a good chance to hear folk songs and see traditional dances.

The Skansen Folk Dance Team performs and fiddlers play traditional tunes for the ring dances around the maypole and for the singing that follows. Folk dance displays continue into the evening and everyone dances on Skansen's outdoor dance floors.

More intimate parties go on at some country inns, especially at Grinda Wardshus, the island country house on Grinda (see page 135), in the archipelago. You can gather wildflowers there and someone will be on hand to show you how to weave a flower crown to wear for the festivities. It's a popular place, so reserve early for that weekend (Ⓦ www.grindawardshus.se).

🔺 *Wildflowers are woven into a crowing glory at Midsummer festivities*

History

While the Vikings had a thriving city on the nearby island of Birka at the turn of the second millennium, Stockholm's history begins in 1252 when Birger Jarl began building Tre Kronor fortress. The city continued to grow, with a setback from the plague in the mid 14th century, until Sweden's entry into the Kalmar Union, which united all four Scandinavian states. Rebellion followed rebellion as the Swedes fought to be free of this Danish domination, including the infamous Stockholm Bloodbath of 1520, when the Danish king beheaded more than 80 leaders of this opposition.

Finally, three years later, Gustav Vasa defeated the Danes and became King of the newly-freed Sweden. But the Danes didn't give up so easily, and the wars continued on and off for decades. Meanwhile, Protestantism took hold in Sweden, and the state confiscated the monasteries and church property. Throughout the 1600s, Stockholm expanded, spilling over onto more islands, but the Great Northern War, against an alliance of most of its neighbours, resulted in the loss of much of Sweden's territory. While this was going on, Parliament reduced the power of the king, creating a parliamentary state. By the end of the 1700s, King Gustav III had restored the crown's power, which got him shot at a masquerade ball, and Parliament regained control.

The middle of the 19th century was a difficult time for Sweden, with economic depression prompting great waves of emigration to the USA and a major movement of rural Swedes into Stockholm. Sweden managed to retain neutrality as World War I raged through the rest of Europe, while political unrest at home resulted in universal voting right, first for men, and soon afterward for women. In World War II, Sweden again remained officially neutral, although

it allowed Nazi forces to cross the country on their way to defeat and subdue Norway.

In the 1950s city officials, as part of their plan to make Stockholm a modern city, began the T-bana underground transit system, and with this as an impetus (some say excuse) they began a systematic destruction of historic neighbourhoods, which were replaced with severe concrete buildings. Now widely agreed to have been a mistake, this wholesale destruction changed the face of Stockholm even more dramatically than the wars had changed other European cities. Massive protests finally succeeded in blocking further destruction in 1975, sparing those parts of the city that had remained undamaged.

By this time other social and political changes were afoot. The monarchy was finally stripped of all political power in 1974, and an enormous wave of immigration to Sweden that had begun in the 1960s began to create social problems undreamed-of in hitherto homogeneous Sweden. In 1995 Sweden joined the EU, following a serious economic depression and devaluation of the Kronor.

Today, with the economy stabilised and thriving, Sweden continues to cope with the serious tax burdens of its welfare state, but takes justifiable pride in a healthy population and progressive policies in dealing with social, environmental and cultural issues.

Lifestyle

While not all Swedes are tall blondes, one of the first things that strikes the visitor is Stockholm's homogeneous population. About 90 per cent of the people who live there are Swedes and 3 per cent are Finns, so the racial and ethnic mix that characterises so many European cities is missing. That is not to say that everyone looks alike, thinks alike or behaves the same. Nor does it mean a narrow-minded attitude toward differences.

● *Enjoy an alfresco lunch (in the warmer months) in one of the city's cafés*

Quite the opposite is true, in fact. Stockholm is well known as one of Europe's most 'live and let live' cities, with an open gay and lesbian scene and an anything-goes nightlife marred only by archaic laws concerning dancing in bars.

Although all this might make the city sound wide open, it is really quite orderly. It is also one of Europe's safest cities, largely because of the Swedish respect for moderation and 'the way things should be' and their high-mindedness about the public good. Not only does Stockholm have a low crime rate (even in the underground transit system), but its air is clean and its waters unpolluted.

If Stockholm is refreshingly free of the seedy underbelly of so many cities, its opposite is also missing. Nothing here seems over the top or simply outrageous, perhaps because of the ingrained Swedish sense of *lagom*. The word translates roughly to 'only enough' – and it underlies the national appreciation of understatement, restraining the temptation to be ostentatious in any way.

So while Stockholm residents play hard – and sometimes drink too much – they are basically well behaved and respectful of each other, of visitors, and of differences.

Gays and lesbians are welcomed officially with the brochures, *Stockholm Gay Map* and *Stockholm Queen of Cities*, which is downloadable at Ⓦ www.stockholmtown.com. The city's Gay Pride celebration in late July or early August is the largest of its kind in Scandinavia. The free newspaper *QX* is a good source of events information, as is their website, Ⓦ www.qx.se.

Perhaps more even than the shared sense of *lagom*, the glue that holds Stockholm society together is coffee. The coffee break is a national institution, and cafés are alive and well – everywhere you look. People seem to stop for a cup on their way to meet a friend for coffee.

Culture

Stockholm's cultural life is rich and varied, with something for all tastes, from grand opera to cutting-edge contemporary art. And even the most high-brow event is not reserved for the rich and privileged.

Classical music and opera fans can go wild in Stockholm, where heavily-subsidised ticket prices are among the lowest in Europe, and hundreds of concerts each year are free. The season for the Kungliga Operan (Royal Opera House) is September to May and for the philharmonic and symphony orchestras at Stockholms Konserthus is August to June. In the summer, seek outdoor venues for concerts and music festivals. The Royal Opera House is also the stage used for the Royal Ballet, which usually performs traditional ballet classics. For more edgy and contemporary operas and avante-garde productions, look to the Folkoperan. Two major theatres also have full schedules, but most of their performances are in Swedish.

For up-to-date listings of performance schedules, see the free booklet *What's on Stockholm*, available at hotels and tourist offices, or look at the events listings by month on the city's tourism website, ⓦ www.stockholmtown.com.

Tickets are available on-line through websites of individual venues, and occasionally at Kulturhuset ⓐ Sergels Torg 1 ⓣ 08.506.20200.
Stockholms Konserthus ⓣ 08.786.0200, ⓦ www.konserthuset.se
Kungliga Operan ⓣ 08.24.8240, ⓦ www.operan.se
Folkoperan ⓣ 08.616.0750, ⓦ www.folkoperan.se

Along with performing arts and music, Stockholm is filled with visual arts, from outstanding public sculpture to its art museums and galleries.

◗ *Carl Milles' impressive* Orpheus *welcomes you to Stockholms Konserthus*

Design is an obsession with the Swedes, a preoccupation highlighted in 2005, which was officially designated a design year. Exhibitions, programmes, newly commissioned works, catalogues and other initiatives spotlighted contemporary designers and artists. The initiative has had a lasting effect in heightening awareness of the unique role Sweden has played in the world of design for many years.

The neighbourhoods of Östermalm and Södermalm have the heaviest concentrations of art galleries, and the new gathering point for emerging artists is in Hornstull, at the western edge of Södermalm. Traditionally, galleries close in summer, reopening in mid August. For news on galleries, openings and shows, look for a copy of *Konstguiden* or check their website, Ⓦ www.konsten.net. It's in Swedish, but the essentials of listings are not too difficult to decipher.

ABBA

The whole world knows Abba, the pop group that burst onto the scene in the 1970s by winning the Eurovision Song Contest with *Waterloo*. At the height of their stride in the late '70s they were Sweden's biggest export, exceeding even Volvo. Although they disbanded in 1983, their popularity continues, their 350 million record sales and continued placement on the UK charts 20 years later making them second only to the Beatles in all-time popularity. They remain the epitome of '70s style, the quintessence of glam pop. In 2005 the group appeared together in public for the first time since 1986, for the Swedish premier of their musical hit *Mamma Mia*.

◗ *Nightime lends a particular enchantment to this maritime city*

MAKING THE MOST OF Stockholm

MAKING THE MOST OF
Stockholm

Shopping

Swedish design is known for innovation and flair, and the graceful beauty of Swedish glassware has made names like Orrefors and Kosta Boda familiar worldwide. Along with design items (for the newest from young unknowns, browse DesignTorget), traditional Nordic jumpers are less expensive here than at home. Knitters excel at well-designed caps and hats, often in striking colours, and children's styles that are clever and practical. Prices on outdoor equipment are good in this land where everyone looks as though they competed in biathlons every Sunday morning.

Hand-forged knives, works of art with carved wood or bone handles (pack them in check-through baggage), are another good, though pricey bet. Bo Bergman is a name to seek. Look for Kalikå in Södermalm and elsewhere for puppets and marionettes, costumes and beautifully-made cookware and shop tools scaled for small hands. Children (and many adults) are fascinated by Norsemen, so consider Viking books, replicas and models.

Stockholm's main shopping streets spread from Hötorget to Gamla Stan, centreing along Drottninggatan, along Kungsgatan to Stureplan and the length of Birger Jarlsgatan. Gamla Stan attracts tourists with boutiques, antique stores and craft galleries, while Södermalm draws Stockholm's young and hip to streets adjoining Götgatan for the right outfits to wear to the nearby bars and clubs.

NK is THE department store, with all the big designers, and P.U.B. is a collection of smaller shops on the Hötorget. This square is filled with market stalls with bargains on everyday needs. Shop hours are fairly standard, 10.00–18.00 Monday through Friday and 10.00–15.00 on Saturday. Many stores, especially in the shopping complexes such as NK, Åhléns and PUB, also open on Sundays, extending hours on weekends.

Sweden's whopping 25 per cent VAT supports its famously broad social programmes, and if you are from an EU country, be prepared to contribute to it yourself. If not, ask for a VAT refund form whenever the total exceeds SEK200 at any shop. When you leave Sweden, take the items and invoices to the airport customs desk for validation. On arrival home, send these invoices to each store for your tax refund. Each cheque will come in Swedish currency and may well cost you more than its value to cash or deposit. Much easier is Global Refund Service. Ask for a refund cheque at any shop displaying a 'Tax Free' logo. At the airport, have these stamped at the Global Refund Desk and collect your refund in cash.

USEFUL SHOPPING PHRASES

What time do they open/close?
När öppnar/stänger?
Nar urp-nahr/stehng-ehr?

How much is it?
Hur mycket kostar det?
Her mewkeh koster deh?

I'd like to buy ...
Jag skulle vilja ha ...
Yer skulleh vilyer hah ...

Eating & drinking

Don't believe the old stereotypes of Scandinavian cooking. Hot young chefs have donned the toques, fusing highly flavourful local ingredients with cooking styles pulled from all over the world. The short growing season and long summer daylight hours intensify the flavours of berries and vegetables, elevating the humble potato to new heights and turning strawberries into juicy sweets.

Swedish chefs shine brightest with garden-fresh vegetables and the readily available coldwater fish and shellfish from surrounding seas. Add autumn woodland mushrooms, wild lingon berries and cloudberries from the northern bogs, as well as venison – the red meat of choice – and you have the basics of Swedish cuisine.

Inventive, innovative Swedish chefs working with these traditional ingredients have led the way in creating a new Nordic cuisine. Stockholm has its share of celebrity chefs, each with a devoted following. Names to note are Erik Lallerstedt at Erik's Gondolen, Johan Lindqvist at Spring, Mathias Dahlgren at Bon Lloc and Pontus Frithiof, chef/owner of Pontus at the Greenhouse. Tina Nordstrom has brought the flavours of the contemporary Swedish

PRICE RATING

The restaurant price guides used in the book indicate the approximate cost of a main course for one person, at the time of writing.

K up to SEK100   **KK** SEK100–200   **KKK** more than SEK200

● *The city's leading restaurants mix traditional dishes with more modern cuisine*

table to world television in her popular series *New Scandinavian Cooking*.

The wave of foreign immigration into Sweden in the 1960s changed Stockholm dining forever. New flavours from the Middle East and Mediterranean crept in and were soon blended with northern ingredients with brilliant results. More recently chefs began incorporating Asian techniques, especially in preparing the abundant local seafood. In fashion-conscious Stockholm, it's all about trendy, so expect anything.

CUTTING KRONORS

Above all, expect to pay for it. Dining in Stockholm can put a dent in your budget the size of a Volvo. Fortunately, the continental brasserie-style has taken hold recently, easing the budget strain a little. The best time to sample the most glamorous places is at lunch, when most offer a fixed-price meal. The sign will advertise a *Dagens Ratt*, or sometimes *Dagens Lunch*.

Main dishes at dinner usually range around SEK100–400 (Asian as low as 65), or SEK275–1200 for set menus. As in most cities, Stockholm's trendier in-spots with designer décor and celebrity chefs are among the priciest, and the neighbourhood places and Asian or Middle Eastern restaurants are the cheapest.

Cafés serve sandwiches and some have all-you-can-eat buffets at lunch. Shopping in markets for picnic foods to take to the park is somewhat difficult, since the food markets in the city centre tend toward gourmet delicacies. But the occasional sandwich shop offers takeout, and you can buy bread and cheese at the Hotorshallen or Östermalms Saluhall markets or in the supermarkets under major departments stores.

THE MENU

A la carte menus offer starters (*forratter*), main courses (*varmratter*) and desserts (*desserter*). Many restaurants offer a set menu both at lunch – usually at a special price – and in the evening.

Traditional local dishes include several varieties of pickled herring, blackened herring (*stromming* or *sill*) with potatoes, salmon (*lax*),

USEFUL DINING PHRASES

I would like a table for ... people, please
Ett bord för ..., tack.
Eht boord fur ..., terk.

May I see the menu, please?
Kan jag få se menyn, tack?
Kern yer for see mehnewn, terk?

I am a vegetarian.
Jag är vegetarian.
Yer air vehgehteriahn.

Where is the toilet (restroom) please?
Var är toaletten?
Vahr air toahlehtehn?

May I have the bill, please?
Jag skulla vilja betala räkningen.
Yer skulleh vilyer beh-tahl-er rairkningehn.

cured salmon (*gravlax*), cod (*torsk*), meatballs (*kottbullar*), and roasted game meats. Occasionally found on menus, a popular home-style dish known as Janssons Temptation (*Janssons frestelse*) includes potatoes, onions, butter, anchovies and cream baked together.

DRINK

Wines and spirits are notoriously expensive (although not as high as they were before Sweden joined the EU). The most low-brow wine in a restaurant can cost ten times more than its shelf price in the UK or US. Nor is a beer the cheap alternative at upwards of SEK30 a glass. The proper drink with the ubiquitous herring or gravlax is schnapps (*brannvin*), which balances the salty-vinegar flavour of the fish.

◆ *Many cafés and restaurants offer good value fixed price menus for lunch*

PRACTICAL DETAILS

Even in the capital, locals dine relatively early, reserving their tables for as early as 18.00, although 19.00 is more common in upper-end places. Restaurant kitchens normally close at 23.00; cafés stay open later. Many restaurants close on Monday and Tuesday, and often for a holiday in July.

Book ahead – as much as a week in advance for popular restaurants – especially for Friday and Saturday evenings. Looking to eat in one of the hottest trend-spots? You're more likely to get a reservation in the days preceding the 25th of the month, Sweden's traditional payday.

Most restaurants accept major credit cards, although smaller ones may accept only cash. Tipping is appreciated, but a service charge is factored into the bill. A 10 per cent tip is considered appropriate for good service. All restaurants in Sweden are non-smoking, by law.

Entertainment & nightlife

BARS, CLUBS & PUBS

Whatever floats your boat, from Abba to Zydeco, you'll find it in Stockholm. You can chill out in the Ice Bar, hear hot jazz at Fasching or Lydmar, hip hop to a DJ in Berns bar, catch edgy choreography at Moderna Dansteatern, mix and mingle at Torget, dance until sunrise at Koket or bravo a world-class tenor at the Opera House. And a lot more besides.

On the current scene, upbeat balladeer Hakan Hellstrom is enormously popular, and chances are you'll hear the lyrical sounds from one of his two albums in bars and cafés. Tummel, a mostly Swedish group, has taken traditional Klezmer music off the shelf, adding some new sounds. The Similou is a spicy discopop/synthpunk duo you'll hear everywhere and The Chrysler is a relatively new Swedish quartet that dominates the folk and alternative country scene. And to prove it's a small world after all, Cajun du Nord, a pan-Scan group featuring Swedish Göran Lomaeus on bass and vocals, has made Zydeco a household word. Pop and rock bands have recently become popular again, and you can find live music almost any night at several Södermalm venues.

Sturplan is the entertainment hub. Up-and-coming Södermalm is hottest with younger and alternative sets, with much of the gay/lesbian scene, the rest of which is on Gamla Stan. Although things don't begin to rock until after midnight (Thursday, Friday and Saturday are the nights to prowl), arrive well before 23.00 to avoid the lines. It's not fashionably late, but you'll get in. Södermalm bars begin to close down about 01.00, clubs at 03.00, but the Sturplan scene continues as late as 05.00.

Don't expect an anything-goes attitude toward dress in

otherwise live-and-let-live Stockholm. How you dress may well govern whether you are allowed in by guard-dog bouncers. Ever style conscious, young Swedes dress the part and you should, too, with your smartest, trendiest outfits in the Sturplan milieu, down-dressing for a more retro or boho-chic look in Södermalm. Stockholm's club scene is complicated by the strict – and perplexing – licensing laws. Permission to dance depends on permission to serve drinks and food, which means that many of the DJ bars do not have dance floors. Don't try to make sense of it.

The minimum drinking age is 18, but bars and clubs can set their own limits, which may be as high as 23. Being smartly turned out and attractive makes you 'older', especially if you're female. Expect to pay an admission fee of SEK50–100 at the Sturplan bars on weekends and as the hour grows late.

CLASSICAL MUSIC

Classical music and opera fans can go wild in Stockholm, where heavily-subsidised ticket prices are among the lowest in Europe, and hundreds of concerts each year are free. The season for the Royal Opera is September to May and the philharmonic and symphony orchestras is August to June. In the summer, seek outdoor venues for concerts and music festivals.

To find out what's hot and what's happening, consult the Friday Dagens Nyheter or Aftonblat. Listings are in Swedish, but easy to interpret. More aimed at tourists is *What's on Stockholm*, available at hotels and tourist offices. Tickets can be purchase on line through the websites of individual venues, at Kulturhuset, (🚇 Sergels Torg 1), or reserved from Globen ticket office (🕐 08.600.3400) and picked up at Sweden House. Get rock and pop events tickets from Svala & Söderlund (Kungsgatan 43; 🕐 08.144.935).

Sport & relaxation

Swedes walk, jog, cycle, run, canoe, kayak, swim and work out in health clubs as a regular habit, so finding ways to get some exercise is pretty easy. And when you need to ease the tired muscles, few cities offer spas like Stockholm's.

Walking & jogging

In Stockholm, you'll never walk alone. The abundant walking paths and promenades are well used by everyone from young parents pushing prams to senior citizens keeping fit. The same routes are good for joggers. Norr Mälarstrand skirts the water from City Hall (Stadshuset) to Rålambshov Park on Kungsholmen, or if you're particularly ambitious, you can walk all the way from the City Hall to Drottningholm Palace.

Djurgarden is networked with bosky paths and waterside *wanderwegs*. In Haga Park, north of Normalm and on a T-bana line, Brunnsviken is a lake with a 12-kilometre jogging trail encircling it.

Cycling

Bike paths and lanes crisscross the city, making a bicycle a good way to sightsee and to explore the wooded **Ekoparken** (ⓦ www.ekoparken.com) paths on Djurgarden. Ask at the Stockholm Visitors Centre for the booklet *Att Cykla i Stockholm City* and for rental information. The archipelago boats that carry passengers between the islands also carry cycles, making it easy to spend a day island hopping and cycling. Or join a group for a guided spin around central Stockholm or Djurgarden with City Sightseeing during July and August. A 3-hour tour (about SEK270) leaves at 10.30 daily, and on Fri and Sat evening tours begin at 17.00 (ⓞ 08.587.14020).

The 50-minute bicycle ride from the Stadshuset (City Hall) to Drottningholm Palace is a scenic and easy route along a well-marked bike path.

Paddle Sports

Canoe and kayak (*kano* and *kajak*) rentals are easy to find along the shore, and the use of kayaks is included at some archipelago inns, such as Grinda Wardshus (page 135). Remember that Stockholm's waterways are very busy with power-driven craft and shipping that not only create huge wakes, but also may not be able to alter their course or slow down for paddlers. Unless you are with a guide who knows the waters and the shipping lanes, stick close to the shore.

Golf

About 50 golf clubs are scattered around the Stockholm area, but it's hard for a traveller to play these courses unless they have local friends who are members. To play at these, you must be a club member and have a green card, as well as a handicap of 36 or lower on weekends and busy days.

Even locals are unable to play an occasional casual game at these, so an alternative has sprung up: pay and play courses. Smaller than the members-only clubs and usually not so posh, they provide a low-key place for beginners or those in town for only a few days. **Vidbynäs** is one of these, in Nykvarn (❶ 08.554.906.00. Ⓦ www.vidbynasgolf.se). For information on other courses, visit Ⓦ www.stockholmgolf.se.

Skating

In winter, join the locals on the ice, renting skates at the rink in Kungstradgarden. You can circumnavigate the city on the ice, too, but unless you have a knowledgeable local with you, it's safer to go with a guide from **Sweden House** ❶ 08.789.2490. The **Stockholm Ice Skate Sailing and Touring Club** (Ⓦ www.sssk.se) has information about routes and organised trips. It's essential to check conditions before setting foot on the ice. And never skate alone.

Spas & health clubs

For a workout, or to work out the kinks afterward, Stockholm offers two classy public baths. **Centralbadet** (Ⓐ Drottninggatan 88. ❶ 08.545.21300) is pure turn-of-the-century eye candy, but serious about its facilities, which include a gym, saunas, steam rooms,

and an amazing art nouveau swimming pool. **Sturebadet** (📧 Sturegallerian, Stureplan. ☎ 08.54.501.500), also with an art nouveau pool, is a bit more high tone, with a power-suit clientele sharing the workout room, steam rooms and pool. For those tired of the posturing of muscle-builders at the next machine, **Friskis & Svettis** (📧 Mäster Samuelsgatan 20. ☎ 08.429.7000) has all the bells and whistles, but more of a health-and-fitness mindset that appeals to the rest of us. And for the hot tub with the best view in town, check into the Clarion in Södermalm, where the top-floor spa is free to guests.

● *There are plenty of places to explore around Stockholm using paddle power*

Accommodation

Hotels in Stockholm tend toward the large and the modern, but with some notable exceptions – and with some outstanding modern hotels. Combining history and grandeur with impeccable service, the Grand Hotel is the city's only five-star lodging, while the Clarion in Södermalm and the sibling Nordic Lights and Nordic Sea hotels carry the modern idea of 'art hotels' to new heights. For pure historic charm, look to Gamla Stan for the Lord Nelson and Lady Hamilton, and to the nearby luxury yacht Malardrottningen.

Brochures on B&Bs and camping can be downloaded at Ⓦ www.stockholmtown.com

It is smart to book ahead, either directly with the hotel, on-line (Ⓦ www.stockholmtown.com), by phone (❶ 08.789.2456), or at Hotellcentrallen, in the central train station.

AF Chapman and **Skeppsholmen K** Sea and land hostel accommodations are available at these two adjacent facilities. Very inexpensive but clean, comfortable and friendly; guests must clean their own rooms. Food service is available in the bar. The sea rooms are aboard the striking white three-masted barque *AF Chapman* in the harbour across from the Royal Palace. All ages are welcome. ❸ Flaggmansvagen 8. ❶ 08.611.7155. ❶ 08.463.2266. Ⓦ www.stfchapman.com

Accome Bromma K–KK. Apartment hotels may be the best option for longer trips and business travel. Updated in 2000, the 182 apart-rooms have broadband and other facilities. The suburb of Alvik is about a 10-minute ride to Stockholm's central station. ❸ Vidängsvägen 9, Alvik ❶ 08.471.1000. ❶ 08.471.1970. Ⓦ www.accome.com

PRICE RATING

All are approximate prices for a single night in a double room/two persons during the summer season (usually with breakfast).

K up to SEK750; **KK** SEK750–1500; **KKK** more than SEK1500

Den Röda Båten, **K–KK** Once The Red Boat sailed the Gota Canal and the Vattern but now it is one of two boats that form the hotel and hostel at the Lake Malaren locks into the Baltic, in Stockholm harbour. Walk to the old town or pubs of Södermalm. Hotel cabins have private baths. ⓐ Söder Mälarstrand 6. ⓣ 08.644.4385. ⓕ 08.641.3733. ⓦ www.theredboat.com

Ariston Hotell KK Only a few minutes from Arlanda airport, this small hotel on the island of Lidingö is only 15 minutes from the city by public transport. Inexpensive, it makes a nice alternative to in-city hotels. ⓐ Stockholmsvägen 70, Lidingö. ⓣ 08.544.81300. ⓕ 08.544.81333. ⓦ www.aristonhotell.com

Best Western Wallin Hotel KK In the heart of the city, at the Conference Centre, 300 metres from Hotorget, the hotel's standard rooms are reasonably sized, with TV and other amenities. One of the best priced modern hotels in the city. ⓐ Wallingatan 15. ⓣ 08.506.16100. ⓕ 08.791.5050. ⓦ www.wallinhotel.com

Elite Arcadia Hotel KK An inexpensive hotel close to the central district and public transportation. ⓐ Mariagränd 3. ⓣ 08.442.1680. ⓕ 08.442.1647. ⓦ www.arcadia.elite.se

Malardrottningen KK For mid-20th-century luxury tinged with star-dust, Woolworth heiress Barbara Hutton's yacht is moored at Rirrarholmen within easy walking distance of the Royal Palace, and with fine dining on board. ➌ On the Quay, Riddarholmen, ➊ 08.545.18780. ➐ 08.24.3676. Ⓦ www.malardrottningen.se

Lord Nelson Hotel KK–KKK Modern hotel with cosy rooms, a half-mile from Central Station in the Gamla Stan section. Sauna, massage and pool are on-site. ➋ Västerlanggatan 22. ➊ 08.506.40120. ➐ 08.506.40130. Ⓦ www.lord-nelson.se

Clarion Hotel Stockholm KKK This Clarion is new, modern and filled with enough contemporary Scandinavian art to qualify it as a gallery (ask for the illustrated guide to the collection). Economical singles, and other rooms and suites are all in striking modern décor and supremely comfortable. The hotel has a well-equipped spa with a view over Södermalm from the hot tub. ➌ Ringwagen 98. ➊ 08.462.1010. ➐ 08.462.10 99. Ⓦ www.clarionstockholm.com

Grand Hotel KKK The grand dame of Stockholm hotels sits across from the city's busy harbour in the very cente, a bastion of grace and elegance that doesn't sacrifice warm hospitality. Dine in the Grand Veranda with views of the harbour. Large rooms combine the elegance of the past with all the modcons. Fitness and business centres and free broadband. ➋ S Blasieolmshamnen 8. ➊ 08.679.3500. ➐ 08.611.8686. Ⓦ www.grandhotel.se

Hotel Rival KKK Originally built in 1937, the Rival has been completely renovated into a smart, contemporary hotel with stunningly-appointed rooms. Well located for access to sights, it also

has its own bistro, bar and bakery. All rooms have plasma TV, DVD, CD, wireless and wired internet; parking is available.
ⓐ Mariatorget 3, ⓣ 08.545.78900. ⓕ 08.545.78924. Ⓦ www.rival.se

Nordic Light Hotel KKK One of the most outstandingly modern hotels in the city, it offers an innovative use of light in guest rooms to set the mood. Guests even get to choose their wall image. An outstanding wine bar features rare American wines and the martini bar offers hundreds of options. Next to the Arlanda Express rail link to the airport. ⓐ Vasaplan 7, ⓣ 08.505.63000. ⓕ 08.505.63040. Ⓦ www.nordiclighthotel.se

Nordic Sea Hotel KKK This sister to the Nordic Light is across the street, offering accommodations of the same quality, but inspired by the sea. The rooms have wireless access, TV and other expected amenities. In the hotel is the Absolut Icebar Stockholm, its walls, windows, ceiling, bar and drinkware are all made of ice. ⓐ Vasaplan 2-4, ⓣ 08.505.63000. ⓕ 08.505.63090. Ⓦ www.nordicseahotel.com

The Lady Hamilton KKK The family-owned and antiques-filled boutique hotel is only a few yards from the Royal Palace and the old town of Gamla Stan. Service matches the location. Check their website for specials. ⓐ Storkyrkobrinken 5, ⓣ 08. 506.40100. ⓕ 08.506.40110. Ⓦ www.lady-hamilton.se

Best Western Mornington KKK Modern and uncluttered contemporary Scandinavian design characterise the public and guest rooms of this conveniently located hotel. The bar and restaurant are open late. ⓐ Nybrogatan 53. ⓣ 08.507.33000. ⓕ 08.507.33039. Ⓦ www.mornington.se

THE BEST OF STOCKHOLM

Whether you are on a flying visit to Stockholm or have a little more time to explore the city, its surroundings or slightly further afield, there are some sights, places and experiences that you should not miss. For the best attractions for children, see pages 149–151.

TOP 10 ATTRACTIONS

- **Changing the Guard** Christopher Robin would love it – all that pomp and marching to military band music (see page 105).

- **Gamla Stan** Old – the remnants of Stockholm's medieval heritage – amid the new (see page 102).

- **Ferries to archipelago islands** Island dreams of peace and nature not too far from the city (see page 120).

- **Vasa Ship** Dredged from the mud and restored to reveal its 17th-century glory (see page 89).

▼ *The spire of Riddarholm church dominates Stockholm's skyline*

- **Skansen Park** Sweden in a day, revealed through buildings and living exhibits in a massive open-air museum (see page 89).

- **Stadhuset** The City Hall, where modern architecture was born, and one of the city's landmarks (see page 63). All that, and a tower providing stunning views over Stockholm.

- **Nordic Museum** Cultural overdose, as a collection of over a million artefacts explain the country's traditions and way of life (see page 88).

- **Drottningholm Palace** How the other half regally lived in the residence fit for a king and his family (see page 68).

- **Birka** Real Vikings didn't have horns on their helmets, at this UNESCO world heritage sight (see page 65).

- **Ice Bar** The coolest place in town – not surprising as it is made of ice. Fortunately, capes are provided for customers so there is no need to freeze (see page 77).

Your brief guide to seeing the best that Stockholm has to offer, depending on how much time you have.

HALF-DAY: STOCKHOLM IN A HURRY

If the weather is nice, wander and treat your eyes to all the sights around the watery rim of downtown Stockholm. Begin at the Royal Opera in Kungstradgarden (pick up a map at Sweden House) and follow the water past the Grand Hotel and the white ferries and around the corner by the national Museum, following the line of boats along Nybrokajen to Berzelii Park and Nybroplan. Step inside the Dramatic Theatre to see the lobby, if it's open, then hop on a ferry to Djurgarden to see the Vasa Ship. Take a ferry to Slussen and stroll through the narrow streets of Gamla Stan in the evening, browsing for a place to have dinner. Give in to the urge to stop for coffee in a cosy café or at a sidewalk table at any time.

1 DAY: TIME TO SEE A LITTLE MORE

The half-day route above makes a good beginning for a full day, leaving time to spend the afternoon in Skansen Park. The highlights not to miss there are the historic buildings, which are set along walking routes. These are arranged geographically, so you get a mini tour of the whole country in past centuries. The mid-19th-century village has working artisans, including a baker. If this makes you hungry, you can stay in the old-time mode with a meal at Solliden (see page 100), where they serve traditional Swedish dishes.

2–3 DAYS: SHORT CITY-BREAK

While you could spend a whole day at Skansen alone, there is a great deal more to see in the city. With an extra day you can either visit two or three of the many museums or begin the day on Gamla

Stan to tour the Royal Palace. In that case, plan to remain for the noon-time Changing of the Guard. If the weather is good, you might spend the day visiting either the Viking island town of Birka (see page 65), Drottningholm castle and its gardens, or one of the islands in the archipelago. The ride is as much the purposes as reaching an island. Vaxholm is the closest, but other islands are accessible on a day trip. Or take an afternoon boat to Grinda and stay overnight at Grinda Wardshus (having made reservations, of course) and watch the sunset from their terrace before – or during – dinner (see page 135). If you have enough time, you can kayak around the island before the ferry arrives for the return trip. Or, if you return to Stockholm, and it's late in the week, it might be a good night to hit some nightspots in Södermalm.

LONGER: ENJOYING STOCKHOLM TO THE FULL

With more time, and a rented car, you could follow the route of the Gota Canal across the narrow country, stopping in Vadstena and Soderkoping (see page 141) and going on to Gothenburg. Highlights

🔵 *Charming, traditional Scandinavian style*

there include the excellent art museum and the world's largest collection of floating museum ships, at the Marine Centre. In the evening you might catch a show at Liseberg, or just enjoy the rides at what is Scandinavia's biggest amusement park.

Something for nothing

While many cities are decorated by monumental statues, few have such a continuing commitment to public art as Stockholm. And few make their most treasured museum collections of world-famous art available free to the public. This city is one big free art gallery.

Several works of Carl Milles, Sweden's premier sculptor, adorn the city, including his *Orpheus* in front of the concert hall on Hotorget. Contemporary sculptures pop up here and there, and in the newly regenerated western edge of Södermalm, a 600-foot-long wall of colourful mosaic dresses up the buildings facing the lakeside

🔺 *Trace Sweden's influence on building design at the Museum of Architecture*

promenade. At Kulturhuset, on Sergels Torg, you'll find free changing exhibits of art by both Swedish and international artists.

The world's longest art exhibition – more than 60 miles of it – is in the city's underground system, the T-bana. Trains pull into nearly 100 stunning stations, each designed in a different way and by a different artist. In some the lighting creates designs in the ceiling, others have massive 3-dimensional wall murals, others are decorated in tiles or sculpture. Top Swedish artists began competing for these commissions as long ago as the 1950s, and the work still continues. *Art in the Stockholm Metro* is a free brochure that describes the various stations, with information on the artists. Ask at the tourist office about free guided tours of the stations. Those on the Blue Line are the most outstanding.

Three exciting art museums invite the public to visit without charge. The National Museum contains paintings by Rembrandt, Rubens, Degas and other well-know artists, as well as decorative arts from the Middle Ages to modern Swedish design treasures. Across the bridge on the island of Skeppsholmen, the new Moderna Museet, also free, is considered to be one of the top museums of modern art in Europe. Its collections include works by Picasso and Salvador Dali, as well as leading contemporary names. Next door is the Museum of Architecture, whose exhibit hall is chock-full of fascinating exhibits on the country's architecture, including models of buildings from all periods of its history. Excellent interactive stations offer photographs and artistic information in English.

While you're on Skeppsholmen, follow the boardwalk around its perimeter to Stockholmsbriggen. Lining the quay are dozens of historic wooden ships, some of which you can visit. At this professional shipyard, craftsmen are building a traditional wooden ship using authentic mid-19th-century methods and materials.

When it rains

Although Stockholm is such a beautiful city that it would be a shame to miss just strolling around and appreciating its elegant buildings and watery vistas, a rainy day does allow time to visit some of the city's museums. Along with the big – and justly famous – trio of the Vasa Ship, Nordic Museum and the National Museum (any one of which can easily take half a day to peruse at leisure), a rainy day gives a traveller the perfect excuse to explore some little-known treasures. Among these is the fairly new Medeltidsmuseum (Museum of Medieval Stockholm), where a section of 500-year-old city has been painstakingly reconstructed. The musically-inclined would enjoy the Music Museum, with collections of old instruments and enough hands-on toys to keep even an adult occupied. The various museums inside the Royal Palace make a good rainy day choice, too, since they are concentrated closely together. The various state apartments, the Royal Coin Cabinet and a museum that explores the origins of the earlier fortress are all within the palace complex. And a good selection of restaurants is only a few (wet) steps away.

Another occupation for a rainy day is shopping in one of the covered shopping complexes. For high end, visit NK, no longer a true department store but a series of label shops run by top-brand companies. Underneath Sergels Torg is an underground street of shops, including a branch of DesignTorget. If you chose Sturegallerian, in Sturplan, you can even top off your shopping with a sauna, massage or swim at Sturebadet, in the gallery. And any place with more than five or six shops is bound to have a café, where you can join the locals at their most cherished custom, the coffee break.

▶ *For an upmarket, undercover shopping experience, head to NK*

On arrival

TIME DIFFERENCES

Sweden follows Central European Time (CET). During Daylight
Saving Time (late Mar–late Sept), the clocks are put ahead 1 hour.
In the Swedish summer, at 12.00 noon, time at home is as follows:

Australia Eastern Standard Time 20.00, Central Standard Time 19.30,
Western Standard Time 18.00
South Africa 12.00.
New Zealand 22.00
UK 11.00
USA and Canada Newfoundland Time 07.30, Atlantic Canada Time
07.00, Eastern Time 06.00, Central Time 05.00, Mountain Time
04.00, Pacific Time 03.00, Alaska 02.00.

ARRIVING
By air

Most international flights arrive at **Arlanda Airport** (❶ 08.797.6100),
north of Stockholm. Airport coaches leave for the Cityterminalen every
5–10 minutes, taking 35 minutes. Adjacent to Cityterminalen is the
Central Station, where trains connect to elsewhere in Sweden. A one-
way trip costs SEK80, or SEK89 including a bus or underground ticket
in zone 1. Arlanda Express trains leave every 15 minutes (10 mins at
peak hours) and take 20 mins to the central station, costing SEK190
each way (❶ 08.588.89000. ❷ www.arlandaexpress.com). The least
expensive option is by the public transport system, using the
commuter train to Märsta and then catching bus no. 583. Taxis can
take you to the door of your hotel, but cost about SEK450–475. The
major companies have fixed rates, and if you prebook before arrival,

you won't have to stand in a queue (Taxi Stockholm ☎ 08.150.000).

Bromma Airport (☎ 08.797.6800), about 8 km west of Stockholm, handles domestic and some international flights. About 100 km south of the city, near Nyköping, is **Skavsta Airport** (☎ 0155.28.0400), handling both domestic and international flights. Airport coaches to Cityterminalen from Bromma (SEK60) and Skavsta (SEK130) match up to flight schedules (☎ 08.600.1000).

By car

While the city is easier to drive in than most European capitals, a car is more of a liability than an asset. Traffic is not heavy, partly because the locals themselves don't see much point in paying for fuel and parking – both expensive – when public transport is so good and safe. If you do drive in the city, expect delays on the bridges between its various islands. Parking is either in multi-level carparks or on-street. Machines that provide tickets for street parking, accept coins or credit/debit cards. Put the ticket inside the vehicle, visible through the windscreen.

Although Sweden's public transport is excellent – you can reach Gothenburg by direct train in as little as three hours – you may want a car to explore the charming towns along the Gota Canal.

Driving is on the right, so drivers bringing their own autos from the UK should be sure their lights are adapted to right-hand driving. Also, lights should be on at all times. The speed limit is 110kph (70 mph) on motorways; 90kph (55 mph) on dual-carriageways and 50kph (30 mph) in densely settled areas.

By boat

Stockholm has a number of ports which service ferry terminals, cruise ships, or boat services around the archipelago (see page 120).

Many are close to the city centre; those further out usually have public transport connections to the centre of town to cater for arriving vessels.

FINDING YOUR FEET

The overwhelming impression of central Stockholm is that it was designed to be viewed across water. Some of its most striking buildings sit facing the lake or harbour, so that you can admire them full face, in an uninterrupted view. The second impression is how sparkling clean and tidy everything is. This impression is heightened on a clear summer day by the incomparable northern light that has inspired so many artists in this latitude, and even at night by the myriad lights doubled by reflection in the water.

Along with being clean, the city is safe. Even its underground transport system is bright and virtually crime-free. Drivers are normally careful of pedestrians. The greatest risk is in assuming that pedestrians have the right of way when crossing bicycle lanes. Whatever the law may be, cyclists do not willingly stop for those on foot, and consider their lanes sacred. Cross with extreme caution.

ORIENTATION

Although its setting on a series of islands means that Stockholm has no overall plan of grid streets and arteries, it is not difficult to find your way. Each section is named; those you will spend the most time in are Norrmalm and Östermalm (side by side on the 'mainland') and the islands of Gamla Stan, Skeppsholmen and Djurgarden. The latter two are almost exclusively made up of museums, and Gamla Stan is easily recognised by the Royal Palace crowning its hill. For nightlife, you will want to cross through Gamla Stan's old narrow streets to Södermalm.

Stockholm is a supremely walkable city, with boats shuttling back and forth between many of the islands to shorten the distances. A sightseeing tour by boat will help you get a sense of where everything lies and recognise some of the landmarks: the City Hall, Royal Palace, Strandvagen, Riddarholm Church, Kaknas Tower and the Globe Arena.

GETTING AROUND

The modern, fast and safe Tunnelbana (T-bana) system covers the entire city, except for Skeppsholmen and Djurgarden. These can be reached by buses 65 and 47, respectively, and Djurgarden can be accessed by the vintage tram 7 from Norrmalmstorg (☎ 08.660.7700).

Purchase tickets for the Tunnelbana from machines in any station. The number of coupons varies with the length of the ride, but the

---

IF YOU GET LOST, TRY ...

Excuse me, do you speak English?
Ursäkta mig, talar du engelska?
Ew-shehkter mey, tahler doo ehng-ehl-sker?

How do I get to ...?
Hur kommer man till ...?
Hewrr kommehr mern til ...?

Can you show me on my map?
Kan du visa mig på kartan?
Kern doo veeser mey po kahrrtern?

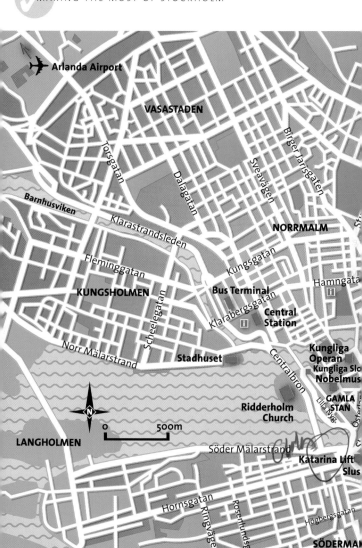

✈ **Arlanda Airport**

VASASTADEN

Torsgatan

Dalagatan

Sveavägen

Birger Jarlsgatan

Barnhusviken

Klarastrandsleden

NORRMALM

Fleminggatan

Kungsgatan

Hamngata

KUNGSHOLMEN

Scheelegatan

Bus Terminal

Klarabergsgatan

Central Station

Norr Mälarstrand

Stadhuset

Centralbron

Kungliga Operan
Kungliga Slo
Nobelmus

Ridderholm Church

GAMLA STAN

Lilla Nyg

Österl

0   500m

LANGHOLMEN

Söder Mälarstrand

Katarina Lift
Slus

Hornsgatan

Ringvägen

Rosenlundsgatan

Högbergsgatan

SÖDERMA

N

Lidingövägen

Naturhistoriska Museet

Valhallavägen

Karlavägen

Sibyllegatan

gardsgatan

ÖSTERMALM

Narvavägen

Oxenstiernsgatan

National City Park

LADUGÅRDSGÄRDET

Kaknästornet

Djurgårdsbrunnsvägen

Musikmuseet

Strandvägen

National Maritime Museum

Tekniska Museet

Junibacken

Nordiska Museet

Vasamuseet

Skansen

SKEPPSHOLMEN

Aquaria Vatten-Museum

DJURGÅRDEN

Djurgårdsvägen

KASTELL-HOLMEN

Gröna Lund

Prins Eugens Waldermarsudde

Baltic Sea

adsgårdsleden

sgatan Folkungagatan

Renstiernas Gata

Nytorgsgatan

machines are easy to operate. Or you can buy a strip of tickets (20 for about SEK120). In either case, you need to have the ticket stamped with a validation as you enter the Tunnelbana. To bypass all the machines, you can buy a pass for free transit: 24 hours (SEK95), or 72 hours (SEK180). For transit information ☎ 08.600.1000.

For hopping between the museum islands and Gamla Stan or Nybroplan, the fastest route is via the little walk-on ferries that shuttle back and forth. The route from Gamla Stan operates year-round; the others are seasonal. Boats heading to Drottningholm Palace, Birka and other points in the western archipelago leave from opposite the Stadshuset (City Hall). A handy hop-on-and-off tour is offered by **Stockholm Sightseeing** (☎ 08.578.14044. ⓦ www.stockholmsightseeing.com), combining a narrated orientation with stops at the five major attractions areas for about SEK100 a day.

Ferries connect the major islands of the archipelago, most leaving from Strandvagen. **Cinderella Boats** (☎ 08.587.14000. ⓦ www.cinderellabatarna.com) operate several trips each day to Vaxholm, Grinda, Sandham and several others. A five-day archipelago pass, available at the tourist office in Sweden House, allows unlimited boat travel among the islands, good value if you plan much island hopping.

The **Stockholm Card** provides unlimited transport on the Tunnelbana, buses and some ferries, along with free access to more than 70 museums and sights, plus two boat tours and discounts on other tours. Prices are steep – 24 hours is about SEK260, 48 hours SEK390, 72 hours SEK540, so you should consider how many rides and how many museums you can (or want to) pack into a day. Unless you plan to skim through a number of sights each day, a strip of transit coupons and individual admissions might be a better deal.

Tunnelbana/T-bana

Reliable taxis are **Taxi Stockholm** (📞 08.150.000), **Taxi Kurir** (📞 08.300.00) and **Taxi 020** (📞 20.20.20.20), clearly identified by their signs. These are metered, starting at about SEK30. Available taxis have a lighted sign on the roof. Most taxis give discounts to women travelling alone at night, if you ask.

CAR HIRE

All major companies are represented in Stockholm, most with desks at Arlanda Airport. Europcar consistently offers competitive rates (📞 UK 132.422.233, USA 877.940.6900). To compare prices, visit 🌐 www.CarRentals.com. Check car hire rates before making your air reservations, because you can often save with an airline's air-car package.

If you plan to stay in the city before travelling elsewhere, consider picking up the car as you leave Stockholm, instead of on arrival. This saves driving in the city and paying for parking. The minimum age for car hire is 18, and you must present (and carry while driving) your own home drivers license. In addition, you will need to show a credit card, even if you are not charging the car to one.

Before leaving the carpark, be sure you have all documents and that you know how to operate the vehicle. The most immediate problem is for those from left-hand drive countries. Not only are you driving on the opposite side of the road, but you must operate the gears with the wrong hand. In normal traffic, it soon becomes natural as you follow other drivers. But in roundabouts or on dual-lane highways, it is easy to make mistakes. Stay alert and ask a passenger to remind you until it becomes customary.

● *Wandering through the city's picturesque streets is a pleasure*

The centre

Norrmalm is the heart of modern downtown Stockholm, where shops, offices, clubs and theatres share elegant streets with grand hotels, smart restaurants and cafés. It is the city's transportation hub, too, with Central Station, Cityterminalen and T-Centralen together in its middle. The almost-round island of Skeppsholmen hangs out into the harbour, tethered by a single bridge. More bridges lead west to Kungsholmen, and to the north the downtown streets and avenues continue into Vasastaden

SIGHTS & ATTRACTIONS

Just walking along the streets in the area that locals call simply 'The City', with its busy harbour, tidy gardens and variety of architecture, is interesting. Expect plenty of subjects to aim your camera toward.

Harbour
With boats and ships constantly moving throughout its waterways, the whole city is a harbour, but the busiest section surrounds the point of land between Nybroplan and the Kungstradgarden. Ferries, sightseeing boats, floating restaurants and café boats dock here, relieving the formality of the surrounding buildings with their bobbing confusion of colours and shapes. The harbour is always an interesting place to sit and watch the world glide by.

Kungstradgarden
Separated from the Royal Palace by a swath of water, Kungstradgarden forms its disembodied dooryard with a grand sweep of gardens and leafy public space. It was, in fact, the palace's

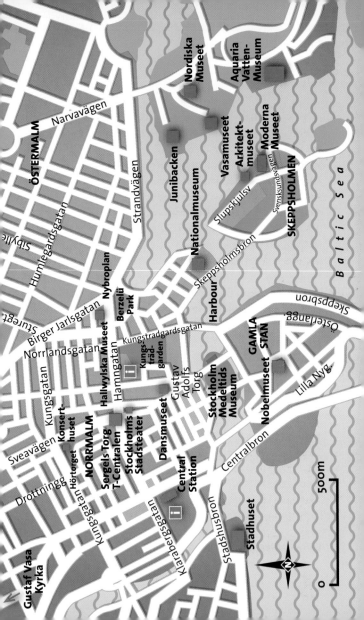

vegetable garden before it was opened to the public in the 1700s. Glasshouse cafés, flower beds, an open-air stage and – in winter – public skating make it into the city's living room. At its far end is Sweden House, with the tourist office and displays of Swedish arts and design.

Kungliga Operan (Royal Opera House)

Elegant and showy enough to contradict the Swedish *lagom* (no more than is necessary) fetish, this hallowed shrine of the high C has a gold-plated lobby nearly 100 feet wide, its ceiling dripping with crystal chandeliers. Jenny Lind, the Swedish Nightingale, began her career here. It houses three restaurants; the Operabaren has a masterpiece *Jugendstil* (art nouveau) interior, worth the price of lunch just to revel in. ⓐ Gustav Adolfs Torg. ⓣ 08.24.8240. ⓦ www.operan.se ⓝ T-bana Kungsradgarden.

Sergels Torg

A good lesson in the pitfalls of levelling a neighbourhood to build a new one is this 1960s eyesore. No one is happy with it, and attempts to make something of the sow's ear (it's unlikely to be a silk purse) have tackled its logistical problems before the considerable aesthetic ones. Towering over it is the glass-walled Kulturehuset, a performance centre and headquarters for all things cultural, from poetry to a library of comic books.

Hotorget

The square north of Sergels Torg is enclosed by larger-than-life buildings that seem to dwarf it. One side is occupied by the PUB

ⓞ *Sergels Torg may draw crowds but it isn't everyone's idea of a city square*

departments store, and another by the columned façade of the Stockholms Konserthus (Concert Hall). This 1926 building is one of the city's few in the art deco style. In the square is an outdoor market with fresh produce and cheap clothing. Here, too, is Hotorgshallen, a food market hall, a bit less toney (and pricey) than the one at Saluhallen.

Centralbadet
An outstanding art nouveau building from 1904 by architect Wilhelm Klemming, the interior and courtyard are worth visiting, even if you don't plan to use its spa or swimming facilities. The interior is beautifully preserved, with stained glass, stenciling,

ornamental metal work and other details in classic art nouveau designs. The exterior facing onto the courtyard also has excellent architectural details, and a quiet garden. ❸ Drottninggatan 88. ❶ 08.545.21300. Ⓦ www.centralbadet.se ❶ Mon–Fri 06.00–22.00, Sat–Sun 08.00–2200, Entrance closes 20.30. Ⓝ T-bana Hotorget; bus 1, 47, 53.

Stadhuset (City Hall)

Perhaps Scandinavia's most admired building, the brick Stadshuset seems to rise directly from the water, at the end of Kungsholmen.

◆ *Art nouveau splendour at the swimming baths – Centralbadet*

Perhaps the best view of it is from the island of Riddarholmen, beyond the Riddarholmskyrkan. The courtyard is open to the public, but the Golden Hall and Blue Hall, where the Nobel prizes are awarded by the king each December, can only be seen on a guided tour (offered in English June–Aug). The Golden Hall depicts scenes from Swedish history in a gold-leaf mosaic of over 18 million pieces. Climb the tower, just shy of 106 m (350 ft) tall, for views across the city. ❸ Hantverkargatan 1. ❶ 08.508.290.59. Tower ❹ May– Sept daily 10.00–16.00. Tours: daily 10.00, 12.00, (Oct–May) daily 10.00, 11.00, 12.00, 14.00, 15.00 June–Aug (English). Admission Charge. ❷ T-bana Centralen, Rådhuset; buses 3, 62.

Boats to Drottningholm and Birka

The dock just in front of the Stadthusset is the boarding place for boats to Drottningholm Palace (page 68) and to the Viking site at Birka (see box right). Boats leave for the palace daily May–Oct at hourly intervals (SEK120 return, combined with palace tickets SEK190). Boats to Birka leave daily May–mid-Sept at 09.30 and again at 13.15 in July and August (SEK225 return includes entrance fee and guides).

Gustaf Vasa Kyrka

The magnificent baroque altarpiece in this early 20th-century church was made for the cathedral in Uppsala in the 1700s, and is well worth venturing into the Vasastaden neighbourhood, north of Norrmalm. Inside the 200-foot-tall dome are frescoes picturing scenes from the New Testament. Frequent organ concerts are held in the church. ❸ Odenplan. ❶ 08.508.886. ❼ www.gustafvasa.nu. ❹ Mon–Sat 11.00–16.00 (times vary with activities and concert schedule), Sun Mass 11.00. ❷ T-bana Odenplan.

BIRKA

Between AD750 and 1050, a Viking settlement flourished on the island of Birka, west of Stockholm, and the ramparts on the hilltop there are the only monumental remains of the Viking world that exist anywhere. This, and the rich finds in more than 1600 grave mounds have made this a UNESCO World Heritage Site. Birka was a trade centre, with rich merchants from Belgium, Holland and France sailing into Lake Malaren to trade goods from Europe and the Islamic world for furs, and the fine metalwork for which the Vikings were known. Today archaeologists still seek to know more about the culture and life of these people, as they interpret the finds in the graves and village. Excellent tours of the island are lead by these archaeologists, who paint a vivid picture of how the island once looked. A museum illustrates Viking life with models of houses and boats, along with display of items found in the site and in grave mounds. The small gift shop is a good source of books on the Vikings, as well as reproductions of their jewellery and other artifacts. Sweden's largest fleet of Viking ship replicas anchors here, with a shipyard, working blacksmith, sail weavers and other craftsmen working to outfit and repair the ships.

Historic ships

Docked along the eastern shore of the small island of Skeppsholmen are dozens of historic vessels, most privately owned and a few offering sailing experiences to the public. A boardwalk runs the length of this area, which was once a busy shipyard, ending at the dock for the ferry to Djurgarden. The ferry is a much faster route than going by land around Nybroplan.

CULTURE

Skeppsholmen, connected to Norrmalm by a bridge from the end of Stromkajen (near the National Art Museum), has a high concentration of museums. Others are close together, near Kungstradgarden.

Arkitekturmuseet (Museum of Architecture)

This small, but fascinating display hall shows models and photographs of Swedish architectural styles from earliest time through to the present. These are supplemented by excellent interpretive material in English, so you can explore any style and not only learn more about it but find existing examples of it in Stockholm. The shop is equally outstanding, a complete bookshop of art and design books in all languages, with a good selection of gifts. ⓐ Skeppsholmen. ⓣ 08.587.27014. ⓦ www.arkitekturmuseet.se ⓛ Tues–Wed 10.00–20.00, Thur–Sun 10.00–18.00. Admission free. ⓝ Buses 62, 3 Fredsgatan, 65 Skeppsholmen church.

Moderna Museet (Modern Museum)

The entire 20th century to the present is represented, in more than 5000 paintings, sculptures and installations, 25 000 watercolours, drawings and graphics, and around 100,000 photographs by artists including Matisse, Picasso, Klee and Dalí. It is one of Europe's major modern art collections. The light, bright modern building also includes an espresso bar, restaurant and a shop selling art books and prints. ⓐ Skeppsholmen. ⓣ 08.519. 55200.

Ⓦ www.modernamuseet.se Ⓛ Tues–Wed 10.00–20.00, Thur–Sun
10.00–18.00. Admission free to permanent collections.
Ⓝ T-bana Kungsträdgården; bus 65.

Nationalmuseum (National Art Museum)

The more than 16,000 paintings and sculptures represent all schools
and styles from the Middle Ages through to the early 20th century,
with works by Rembrandt, Rubens, Renoir, Goya, Degas and Gauguin
as well as those of the foremost Nordic artists. The French 18th-
century collection is especially well-known for its size and quality.
Applied arts and design collections are strongest in ceramic art (more
than one third of the 30,000 pieces), but contain good glass, textiles,
furniture and metal arts. Ⓐ Södra Blasieholmshamnen.
Ⓘ 08.519.54300. Ⓦ www.nationalmuseum.se Ⓛ Sept–May Tues, Thur
11.00–20.00, Wed, Fri–Sun 11.00–17.00, June–Aug Tues 11.00–20.00,
Wed–Sun 11.00–17.00. Admission charge for special exhibits.
Ⓝ Buses 46, 55, 59, 62, 65, 76; T-bana Kungsträdgården.

Hallwylska Museet

The Hallwyl Palace, facing Berzelii Park, dates from the late 19th
century, and its sumptuous rooms have not been altered since the
1920s, when it was still a private residence. You can step inside to
admire the courtyard, staircases and foyer and to browse in the
shop, or pay to see the next floor unescorted, but the rest of the
palatial home is open only on a guided tour (in English at 13.00).
Designed by the architect of the Nordic Museum, Isak Gustaf
Clason, it was the marvel of moderninity in its day – the first home
in Stockholm with running water, electricity, central heating and
telephones, plus one of the first bathrooms in Sweden. The tour
includes this elegant (for its day) WC, which was heated by an early

sunlamp. ➋ Hamngatan 4. ➊ 08.519.55599.
ⓦ www.hallwylskamuseet.se ➋ mid-Aug–June Tues–Fri 11.45–16.00,
Wed also 18.00–19.00, Sat–Sun 11.30–16.00. July–mid-Aug Tues–Fri
10.45–17.00, Wed also 18-19, Sat–Sun 10.30–17.00. Admission charge.
Ⓝ T-bana Östermalmstorg; bus 46, 47, 55, 62, 69, 76.

DROTTNINGHOLM PALACE

Modelled after Versailles, but much more inviting and far less
pompous, Drottningholm Palace is the residence of the
Swedish royal family. The palace was constructed in the late
1600s, with a second storey added to the wings in the next
century. Drottningholm Slottsteater (Court Theatre), the
pavilion of Kina Slott and the English Park and French formal
gardens were also added in the 1700s. The entire ensemble
was declared a UNESCO World Heritage Site in 1991.

On a tour of the palace interior (with a guide or
independently with a descriptive brochure) you can see the
rooms designed by Nicodemus Tessin the Elder, Sweden's
foremost early baroque architect. These include the
magnificent grand staircase, the Ehrenstrahl Drawing Room
and the dowager Queen's State Bedchamber. Karl XI's gallery
and the elegant library date from later work.

➊ 08.402.6280. ⓦ www.royalcourt.se ➋ May–Aug daily
10.00–16.30, Sept daily 12.00–15.30, Oct–Apr Sat–Sun
12.00–15.30. Admission charge. Ⓝ T-bana Brommaplan,
then bus 177, 178 or several others. Boats and cycling path
from Stadthusset.

Dansmuseet (Dance Museum)

The collections of this interesting museum relate to dance through the ages and around the world, showing everything from African masks to costumes from the Paris Russian and Swedish ballets of the 1910s and 1920s. Watch dance videos, see live lunchtime

Slottsteater (Court Theatre)

Completed in 1766, the theatre is much like a stage set itself, its décor worked in papier mache, stucco and paint. The original Italian stage machinery allows quick scene changes and provides such special effects as moving waves and clouds, wind and thunder. One of only a handful of early European theatres remaining, this one is especially rare for having its original 18th-century stage sets (which have been copied for use in performances) and machinery in good working order. Productions often feature lesser-known operas, focusing largely on French baroque opera. Half-hourly guided tours include a look into this back-stage bag of tricks.
🕿 08.660.8225. 🕔 Mon–Fri 11.00–12.00, 14.00–15.00 for tickets. Tours daily May 12.00–16.00, June–Aug 11.00–16.30, Sept 13.00–15.30. Admission charge. 🌐 www.dtm.se

Kina Slott

A birthday gift for a queen, this pleasure palace, in the form of a red and yellow 'Chinese' pavilion, has curving wings and decorations in a theme inspired by 18th-century notions of China. 🕔 May–Aug daily 11.00–16.30, Sept daily 12.00–15.30. Admission charge.

performances or learn to tango at seasonal Saturday classes.
🅐 Gustav Adolfs Torg 22. 🕿 08.441.7650. 🌐 www.dansmuseet.se
🕐 June–Aug Mon–Fri 11.00–16.00, Sat–Sun 12.00-16.00, Sept–May
Tues–Fri 11.00–16.00, Sat–Sun 12.00-16.00. Admission free (charged
for special exhibitions). 🚍 Buses 43, 47, 62, 69.

Stockholms Medeltidsmuseum (Museum of Medieval Stockholm)
In the 1970s, archaeological excavations unearthed remains of
Stockholm dating from the Middle Ages, and this museum was built
to protect and interpret them. A section of 16th-century city wall is
intact, with nearby homes and artisans' shops, harbour and even
gallows authentically reconstructed to give a sense of what the city
was like half a century ago. You can see the Riddarholm Ship, listen
to a medieval choir and see how medieval buildings were
constructed. Special exhibits bring various events, people and
medieval times to life. 🅐 Strömparterren, Norrbro. 🕿 08.508.31808.
🌐 www.medeltidsmuseet.stockholm.se 🕐 Sept–June Tues–Sun
11.00–16.00, Wed 11.00–18.00, July–Aug Thur–Tues 11.00–16.00, Wed
11.00–18.00, Guided tours daily 14.00. Admission charge.
🚍 Buses 43, 62.

RETAIL THERAPY

The city's premier department stores are in Norrmalm, along with
street after street of shops and underground galleries lined with
even more. Kungsholmen is an up-and-coming neighbourhood for
shopping, less pricey and a bit less predictable.

Åhléns For trendy fashion – both Swedish and international – or a
little something to decorate your flat, this department store has it.

Music and food share the lower level. The day spa is pure luxury.
ⓐ Klarabergsgatan 50. ⓣ 08.676.6000. ⓦ www.ahlens.com

Design Torget is the place to see and buy the latest in Swedish design

Design Torget Be the first to see and buy what's new and cool from the hottest designers and from students who haven't made their name yet. You may find anything from paperclips to furniture here, but it will always be fresh and very SwedeSmart. Kulturhuset (lower level), 🚇 Sergels Torg. ☎ 08.508.31520.

Hötorgshallen Food purveyors sell imported goodies and local ingredients in a busy market milieu. 🚇 Hötorget. ☎ 08.230.001.

NK (Nordiska Kompaniet) Five storeys of haute everything, richly displayed in a *Jugendstil* building, NK is a destination and an attraction as much as a shopping experience. Ladies – and not a few men – lunch on the top floor, and the lower floor is a food emporium. For all its grandeur, it's not intimidating to shop here. 🚇 Hamngatan 18-20. ☎ 08.762.8000.

Gallerian Freshly updated (and upgraded) with needed facelift and a few tucks, Gallerian is no longer the frumpy auntie. New shops bring a new look, with Puma Concept, Gate One, H&M and their likes filling the 8,000-square-metres of shopping space. Axelsons, a mini-spa is there if you should shop 'til you drop. 🚇 Hamngatan 37.

Stockhome Everything your Euro-chic living space needs, in sleek modern designs. Refurnish your kitchen with glassware and dishes, choose cool new towels, or redo the nursery. If they're clever enough to come up with the perfect name for the store, you can trust their choice of stuff to fill it with. 🚇 Kungsgatan 25. ☎ 08.411.1300.

Beneath Urban design for the too-cool man. Beneath has top labels from Adam Lemner to Z, but so few of each that you needn't worry

● *The stylish, upmarket NK is a mustn't-miss retail experience*

about meeting yourself at the bar. ⓐ Kronobergsgatan 37,
Kungsholmen. ⓣ 08.643.1250.

TAKING A BREAK

Cafés are a local institution, places to indulge of the national
pastime of drinking coffee and chatting with friends. The posher
ones serve sumptuous teacakes and pastries. When you need a

respite from shopping and sightseeing, this part of town offers the ultimate old-fashioned spa with a café and garden, as well as waterside parks for quiet repose.

Centralbadet Full of character and serving fresh, healthy lunches and snacks, this glorious art nouveau bath house has its original 1904 interior of stained-glass panels and stencilled walls. Munch your grilled focaccio or fresh fruit salad at café tables in or out in the secluded garden. You may be tempted to take a longer break, and spend the afternoon relaxing in the spa. ➌ Drottninggatan 88. ➊ 08.545.21300. ⓦ www.centralbadet.se ◗ Mon–Fri 06.00–22.00, Sat–Sun 08.00–22.00, Entrance closes 20.30. Ⓝ T-bana Hotorget; bus 1, 47, 53.

Grand Veranda On June 14, 1974, the Grand Hotel celebrated its 100th birthday by opening a permanent version of the seasonal cafés they had constructed for each of their hundred summers. The Grand Veranda continued the fine tradition, but could be open year round, so now Christmas shoppers can enjoy their lunch with the same beautiful view across the harbour, Old Town and Royal Palace that summer visitors revel in. This is THE place to meet, and its smorgasbord, served at lunch May through August (and evenings year-round), is simply the best. ➌ Sodra Blasieholmshammen 8. ➊ 08.679.3586. ⓦ www.grandhotel.se ◗ Daily 07.00–23.00.

Max If you have a hunger that only a burger can fill, head for the nearest shop in Sweden's oldest fast food chain for a Maxburger or a Max Deluxe. ➌ Hamngatan at Kungsträdgården. ➊ 08.611.3810.

Vete-Katten Very old-school European, in the grand manner,

Vetekatten is the terribly genteel choice for coffee and a little bit of something overlooking the park. ⓐ Kungsgatan 55. ⓣ 08.218.454. ⓦ www.vettekatten.se

Norrlands Bar & Grill Good food, reasonable prices and a mellow, friendly atmosphere for a beer or snack. ⓐ Norrlandsgatan 24, Stadsde. ⓣ 08.545.06240.

Tranan Below the restaurant is a basement bar with a very mixed clientele in the after-work hours. It's cool without trying too hard, a nice vibe. ⓐ Karlbergsvägen 14, Vasastaden. ⓣ 08.527.28100. ⓝ T-bana Odenplan.

Cliff Barnes You'll remember this friendly bar, so laid back that sometimes they don't collect your money. Just drop it into the honour-system box as you leave. ⓐ Norrtullsgatan 45. Vasastaden. ⓣ 08.31.8070. ⓝ T-bana Odenplan.

Martins Gröna Only two dishes to choose from each day, and only at lunch, but the prices are very low for generous servings of delicious vegetarian dishes. You may have to wait for a seat, but it's worth it. ⓐ Regeringsgatan 91. ⓣ 08.411.5850.

Mälarpaviljongen If the day is nice, take your coffee al fresco and watch the boats go by. After the shops close, this is a popular place to watch the sun set with an aquavit. They serve food, as well. ⓐ Norr Mälarstran, Kungsholmen. ⓣ 08.650.8701.

Muffin Bakery Muffins aren't the only tasty things here; warm soups, salads and sandwiches are on the menu. Just try to get out

without humming 'Have You Seen the Muffin Man' – it's almost impossible. ⓐ Fridhemsgatan 3, Kungsholmen. ⓣ 08.518.00.

AFTER DARK

As the offices and shops begin to close, the bars come alive. That scene segues into dinner and then – on Thursday, Friday and Saturday nights – to the clubs. Things don't really pick up clubwise until after midnight. While not as haute-brow as neighbouring Stureplan, Norrmalm is decidedly not the place to dress down.

Bars & clubs

Absolut Ice Bar Talk about cool, this place is frigid. The hefty price includes the Star-Wars silver cape with faux-fur hood, thick gloves and mukluks, all of which you'll welcome even after a hot day. Drinks are all Absolut-ly chilled and served in chunky crystal glasses – ice crystal that is, frozen from pure arctic water from Lapland. So are the walls, the bar and even the art. Try the Ice Bear, made with blueberry liqueur, elderflower juice and blue Curacao with Absolut Vanilla. ⓐ Nordic Sea Hotel, Vasaplan 2-4. ⓣ 08.505.63000. ⓦ www.nordicseahotel.se ⓛ year-round, until 24.00, Sun 22.00. ⓝ T-bana Centralen.

Berns One of the city's oldest institutions – and hottest hangouts, with live music, bars and a classy restaurant (**KKK**). One of the city's oldest institutions – and hottest hangouts, with live music, bars and a classy restaurant. It's the darling of Stockholm's yuppies, who don't blanch at the price tag and appreciate that not just anyone

---

◐ *Absolut Ice Bar is so icy cool that you'll need a hat and gloves*

can get in (except on a slow night). Dress well, and you'll dance to anything from techno-house and grime to R&B. Berzelii Park 9. 08.566.32222. www.berns.se T-bana Kungsträdgården.

Dry Martini Bar Choose your time here, carefully planned to be quiet and sophisticated for the after-work crowd, a bit more chic 60' style at higher volume for the about-to-go-outs, and after 10 up-tempo and decibels for 20-somethings. The bartenders claim they can serve 202 varieties of martini, so whatever slakes your gin-and thirst, you're sure to find it, and a few more. You'll also find the most fashionable people here, working their way through the list. Tough work, but somebody's got to... Nordic Light Hotel, Vasagatan 11. 08.505.63000. Open until 01.00. T-bana Centralen.

Fasching The city's best club for jazz, popular with a younger/older, local/foreign, mixed crowd that makes it refreshingly interesting. The range of jazz is all-encompassing, with Dixieland, modern, Afro, Latin and cool. Kungsgatan 63. 8 534 829 64. www.fasching.se Open Mon–Sat, until 04.00 Fri–Sat. T-baba Kungstradgarden.

Nalen Like all Stockholm nightspots with dancing, Nalen has a restaurant and bar along with its two stages. The shows and events can be anything from Swedish comedy to punk, frequently big-name. Some are free, some very pricey. Tickets go on sale one hour before shows. Regeringsgatan 74. 08.505.29200. T-bana Hotorget; bus 2, 42, 43, 44.

Stacy The popular late-night club offers R&B, reggae, raga and more, with lots of room. Regeringsgatan 61. 08 411 59 00. T-bana Hotorget; bus 2, 42, 43, 44.

Restaurants

India Curry House K–KK Very small, very good and very popular. No surprises, except maybe that Indian food can be this authentic this far from India. Expect to wait for a table. ➌ Scheelegatan 6, Kungsholmen. ☎ 08.650.2024. Ⓝ T-bana Radhuset.

KB Restaurant and Bar KK To brush elbows with the actors you may see on stage another night, join the arts set at their favourite hangout for several generations. The food is classic Swedish cooking – not always an easy thing to find in trendy Stockholm – and always good. Look up at the highly theatrical art nouveau façade before you enter. ➌ Smålandsgatan 7. ☎ 08.679.6032. Ⓝ T-bana Ostermaalmstorg.

Prinsen KK Art and artists are central themes, the walls covered in paintings and the booths filled with writers and artists. Dine on traditional dishes, especially the herring, along with some more avante garde choices. ➌ Mäster Samuelsgatan 4. ☎ 08.611.1331. ◷ daily lunch and dinner. Ⓝ T-bana Ostermaalmstorg; bus 2, 5, 56, 69.

Rolfs Kök KK A good choice for solos, who can eat at a companionable bar with a view of the open kitchen to amuse them. The menu is as modern as the décor, with fusion reigning supreme in dishes such as fish ragoût with parmesan and basil cottage cheese. The daily lunch special is always a good bet. ➌ Tegnérgatan 41. ☎ 08.587.14000. Ⓦ www.rolfskok.se ◷ Daily, Sat–Sun evening only. Ⓝ Buses 40, 57, 52, 65.

Grill KK–KKK The atmosphere strives to be that of a modern living room, where guests can relax. Prepare to be surprised by the innovative choices, such as foie gras BLT with corn brioche and ginger, grilled venison ribs with ancho chilli, apple and pumpkin. Every plate, even desserts, has something grilled. 📍 Drottninggatan 89. 📞 08.314.530. 🖥 www.grill.se 🕐 Mon–Fri 11.30–14.00, 17.00–01.00, Sat 17.00–01.00, Sun 16.00–01.00. 🚌 Buses 40, 57, 52, 65.

Halv Trappa plus Gård KK–KKK Chinese (they turn out a fine Szechuan feast) restaurant down, cosy bar up and another outdoors for long summer nights. A trendy crowd drinks to lounge music. 📍 Lästmakargatan 3. 📞 08.678.1050. 🖥 www.halvtrappaplusgard.se 🕐 until 03.00 Wed–Sat, Tues to 01.00.

Light Bar & Lounge KK–KKK The wine cellar at this design hotel is a treasure trove dedicated exclusively to American wines, and they make it possible to sample several of these, accompanied by foods chosen to complement them perfectly. Four tapas-sized dishes are paired with four tasting-sized glasses of wine as combinations, or you can choose both à la carte from a tempting menu that might include foie gras with gooseberry compote, cured breast of wild duck, deep-fried fishcakes with pineapple-chilli salsa or baked fig with walnut, bacon and goat cheese. 📍 Nordic Light Hotel, Vasagatan 11. 📞 08.505.63000. 🕐 until 01.00. 🚇 T-bana Centralen.

Bon Lloc KKK Consistently rated among Scandinavia's top restaurants, Bon Lloc is the work of one of the country's best-known chefs, Mathias Dahlgren. Dishes are inspired by Mediterranean cuisines, and the ingredients are a skilful blend of local and imported from the sunny Med. Look for the likes of wild tundra game birds in a terrine with Spanish ham, or a starter of lightly grilled tuna with smoky mayonnaise, artichokes and caviar. The wine

list worthy of the menu. ⓐ Regeringsgatan 111. ❶ 08.660.6060.
Ⓦ www.bonlloc.nu ⏰ Mon–Sat 18.00–24.00. Ⓝ Buses 2, 42, 43, 44.

Cafe Opera KKK Of the dining/social venues in the opera house, Café Opera is the most exclusive, with superb service and a Continental clientele. Dress well, and hope for the best; the party begins around 23.00, as does the admission charge. ⓐ Royal Opera, Kungsträdgården. ❶ 08 676 58 07. Ⓝ T-bana Kungsträdgården.

Entertainment
Stockholms Konserthus Classical and symphonic music, often hosting international performers, in an art deco concert hall. ⓐ Hötorget 8, ❶ 08.786.0200. Ⓦ www.konserthuset.se Ⓝ T-bana Hotorget.

Stockholms Stadsteater
Swedish language performances and 'Soup Theatre' with a changing menu of performance and soups daily. ⓐ Kulturhus, Sergels Torg. ❶ 08.506.20200. Ⓝ T-bana Centralen.

Kungliga Operan (Royal Opera House)
Past the expansive gold-plated lobby is a splendid opera theatre. Generous government support makes this one of the most affordable places in Europe to hear and see grand opera performed, by the resident ensemble and touring divas. This is also the home of the Royal Ballet, and on some days two different performances are scheduled. ⓐ Gustav Adolfs Torg. ❶ 08.24.8240. Ⓦ www.operan.se Ⓝ T-bana Kungsradgarden.

Cinema Grand Independent films and art movies are the speciality, usually in their original language. ⓐ Sveavagen 45. ❶ 08.411.2400.

Östermalm & Djurgarden

The smartest streets for shopping and nightlife share this eastern side of the city with Stockholm's eco-valhalla, the leafy island of Djurgarden. This green paradise with its scrollwork of winding lanes is the perfect antidote to Östermalm's obsession with the chic and trendy. Walk or bike through its gardens, enjoy the water-framed views of the city and explore its museums at leisure. Some of the city's most outstanding attractions are located on Djurgarden, so allow plenty of time to enjoy them.

SIGHTS & ATTRACTIONS

The line between Östermalm and Norrmalm is a blurry one, but for practical purposes Östermalm begins with the tres-chic shopping boulevard of Birger Jarlsgaten. Anchoring the neighbourhood's southern end is the stunning row of *belle époque* buildings along Strandvagen – itself a mecca for the well-heeled shopper. Facing onto Nybroplan, where these two streets meet, Stockholm's showiest bit of architecture, the Royal Dramatic Theatre, sets the tone for the streets that lie beyond it. Welcome to Stockholm at its most rarified.

Kungliga Dramatiska Teatern (Royal Dramatic Theatre)
Art nouveau shot over the top in this theatre, built at the height of Scandinavia's fascination for the style, between 1902 and 1908. One of the city's most striking buildings (especially with the late afternoon sun setting fire to the two gold lamp posts at the front), the theatre is where Greta Garbo, Ingrid Bergman and Pernilla August all learned their art. Inside is a virtual museum of art nouveau, from the marble-faced Marmorfoajén with its huge ceiling

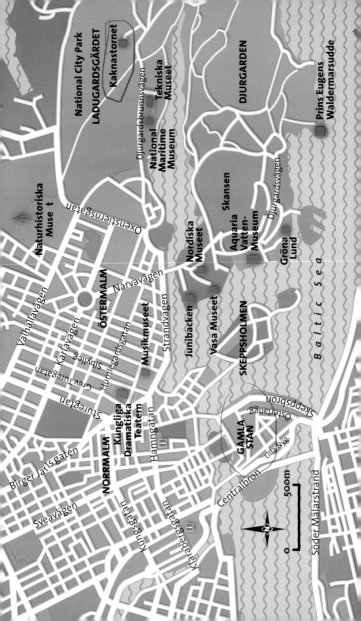

painted by Carl Larsson in the upper foyer, to the round multi-tiered performance hall itself. Tours (call ahead for English, offered only in July) explore the backstage as well as the public areas.

ⓐ Nybrogatan 2, ⓣ 08.665.6115. ⓦ www.dramaten.se ⓝ T-bana red line to Östermalmstorg, Birger Jarlsgatan exit; bus/tram 47, 69,76,7 Nybroplan stop; bus 46, 55 ,62 Norrmalmstorg stop.

◯ *It's worth visiting this theatre even if you aren't going to see a show*

Birger Jarlsgaten

Art nouveau and other elegant styles of the preceding decades decorate the facades of this smart shopping street and the smaller streets leading from it. The fanciful architectural embellishments compete with the contents of the shop windows for an ostentation rare in this land of Nordic reserve. Jugendstil takes a Venetian twist just round the corner of Smolandsgatan, at Number 7.

Just beyond, look into the recently restored turn-of-the-century shopping arcade, Berger Jarlspassagen. This posh avenue leads

straight into the nerve centre of Stockholm's fashionistas, Stureplan.

Junibacken

Astrid Lindgren's lovable character Pippi Longstocking is the star of this kid-centred attraction, where visitors ride a train over rooftops, through houses and across the land of her adventures to do battle with a dragon. Be sure to ask for the narration in English, although the sights and sounds are fun in any language. Allow time for kids to explore Pippi's wacky house and dress up in storybook costumes, as well as play the interactive games and watch special events, such as puppet shows. Characters from other children's classics may visit, and the excellent bookstore is a good place to find gifts to take home to little people. ❸ Galärvarvsvägen, Djurgarden.
❶ 08.587.23000. Ⓦ www.junibacken.se ☾ Open Sept–May Tues–Fri 10.00–17.00, Sat–Sun 9.00–18.00, June, Aug daily 10.00–17.00, July daily 9.00–19.00. Admission charge. Ⓝ Buses 44, 47, tram 7, boat from Nybroplan or Slussen.

Nordiska Museet

You can hardly miss this elegantly adorned building, with its towers rising above the trees of Djurgarden. Hard as it is to believe from its size, this was only a part of the original plan – an entrance hall for the main museum, which would have been twice this size. It was constructed 1889–1907, to a design by Isak Gustaf Clason, architect of the Hallwyl Palace. ❸ Djurgårdsvägen 6-16. ❶ 08.519.54600. Ⓝ Buses 44, 47, tram 7, boat from Nybroplan or Slussen.

Gröna Lund

Stockholm's scaled-down version of Tivoli, but just as sparkling clean and charming as its Danish big sister. The roller coaster offers a split-second view of the city that is breathtaking – literally – just before you drop suddenly earthward. Most of the carousels, Ferris wheels and kiddie rides are vintage pieces, kept in perfect repair since the park's opening over a century ago. Concerts are held here on summer evenings and cafés dot the pretty park.

ⓐ Lilla Allmänna Gränd 9, Djurgården. ① 08.587.50100. ⓑ Open May–Sept, times vary. Admission charge. Ⓝ Buses 44, 47, boat from Nybroplan or Slussen.

Prins Eugens Waldemarsudde

Prince Eugen was King Gustav V's brother, and a talented, prolific artist. His home, a three-storey mansion set facing the water, is a landmark on the Djurgarden shore. Designed by the same architect as the art nouveau NK Department store, the mansion is set in gardens adorned with sculptures by Rodin, and Sweden's own Carl Milles, a contemporary of the prince. Paths lead past a gallery to a large windmill, also overlooking the water. ⓐ Prins Eugens Väg 6. ① 08.545.83700. Ⓦ www.waldemarsudde.se Ⓝ Bus 47.

Kaknastornet (Kaknas Television Tower)

Reputed to be the tallest structure in Scandinavia, this communications tower is certainly the ugliest, looking as though it was built by a toddler from sand-coloured Lego. And you can see it from anywhere in town. The upside is that from its 500-foot elevation, you can see the whole city and as far as the Archipelago, in a sweeping panorama of islands and water. Restaurang Kaknästornet is at the top, for coffee or lunch.

ⓐ Ladugårdsgärdet. ① 08.667.2105. ⓑ Sept–Apr 10.00–21.00, May–Aug 09.00–22.00. Admission charge (free with restaurant reservations ① 08.667.2180. Ⓝ Bus 69.

CULTURE

This island of Djurgarden has the city's highest concentration of museums, anchored by Skansen . This historic assembly preserves homes and buildings from all over the country, making it a journey not only into the past, but into the heart of Sweden itself. Another cluster of museums stands somewhat isolated, near the Kaknas Television Tower, along Djurgardsbrunnsvagen.

Musikmuseet (Music Museum)

Musical instruments – about 6,000 of them from all over the world – are the heart of this museum, but its soul is in the sounds they make. Play with sound in interactive exhibits that aren't just for kids, and in the sound room, while kids create their own noise in the Klåjnk, a musical workshop. Learn more about ABBA here.
ⓐ Sibyllegatan 2. ❶ 08.519.55490. ❷ Sep–June Tues–Sun 12.00–17.00, July–Aug daily 10.00–17.00.

The Nordic Museum (Nordiska Museet)

Swedish culture – everything from its native Sami population and traditional folk arts and costume to table settings and textiles – is presented in attractive interpretive displays. Portable CD commentaries on the collections are available in English. This is a fascinating place, essential to a visitor's understanding of Swedish culture. The collections (which include well over one million pieces) are overwhelming in scope, so the best plan is to skim most, zeroing in on those of particular personal interest. The shop is well worth a stop, too. ⓐ Djurgårdsvägen 6-16. ❶ 08.519.56000. ❷ Mon–Fri 10.00–16.00; Sat–Sun 11.00–17.00. Admission free. Ⓝ Buses 44, 47, tram 7, boat from Nybroplan or Slussen.

Vasa Museet (Vasa Ship Museum)

On her maiden voyage, the Royal Warship *Vasa* sailed less than a mile before sinking in Stockholm's harbour. The year was 1628, and she lay there in the mud until 1961, when she was raised to the surface and the remarkable story of her restoration began. Be prepared for an impressive shock as you step into the darkened building and see this ship, resplendent in restoration, looming above. You can inspect the Vasa Ship at several levels, peering into the gunports (these were open when the ship began to list, allowing water to rush in and tip the vessel farther) and entering the 17th-century seafaring world through displays of shipbuilding, shipboard life and period culture. Begin with the film explaining the history and the salvage process. ⓐ Galärvarvet, Djurgården.
ⓘ 08.519.54800. ⓦ www.vasamuseet.se ⓛ daily 10.00–17.00 (until 20.00 Wed). Admission charge. ⓝ Buses 44, 47, 69, tram 7, boat from Nybroplan or Slussen.

Museifartygen (Museum Ships)

Included in admission to the Vasa Museum are tours to two floating museum ships.

Docked behind the Vasa Museum are two historic boats (which can be viewed from the dock for free). The Icebreaker *Sankt Erik*, Sweden's first sea-going icebreaker, was built in 1915 and the Lightship *Finngrundet* was one of the country's last operating lightships. ⓐ Galärvarvspiren. ⓘ 08.519.54891.
ⓦ www.vasamuseet.se ⓝ Buses 44, 47, 69, tram 7.

Skansen

The concept of open-air museums that gathered together endangered buildings and cultural icons so that later generations could appreciate their roots may have begun on Djurgarden. Opening in 1891, this museum of Swedish folk life and culture is a window into Sweden's past, with more than 150 buildings dating before 1900. The oldest is from the 1400s, and the buildings are arranged geographically according to their origins. Craftspeople demonstrate glassblowing, metal working, wood carving, basketry, weaving and other skills of the past, and you can buy the results in studios throughout the village or at the excellent gift shop at the entrance.

In the Rose Garden grow traditional herbs used for medicines and flavouring, and a small zoo contains examples of Sweden's native animals. Here you can see reindeer, wolves, brown bears, moose, otters and seals. Spread over 75 acres, the sheer size of Skansen means that you could spend most of the day here seeing everything. ⊙ Djurgårdsslätten. ⊙ 08.442.8000. ⊚ www.skansen.se ⊙ May–Sept daily 11.00–17.00, Oct–Apr 11.00–15.00. Admission charge. ⊙ Buses 44, 47, tram 7, boat from Nybroplan or Slussen.

Aquaria Vattenmuseum (Water Museum)

This world of water and the creatures that live in it fascinate children, but it's just as interesting for the rest of us to follow the path of a river from a mountain stream to the sea. Tanks and displays at each stage show what lives there – salmon, tadpoles, bright coral reef fish, even sharks. ⊙ Falkenbergsgatan 2. ⊙ 08.660.4940. ⊚ www.aquaria.se, ⊙ Tues–Sun 10.00–16.30. Admission charge. ⊙ Buses 44, 47.

National Maritime Museum

If you wanted to run away to sea as a child – and haven't really

⊙ *The 17th-century Vasa Ship has undergone an amazing restoration*

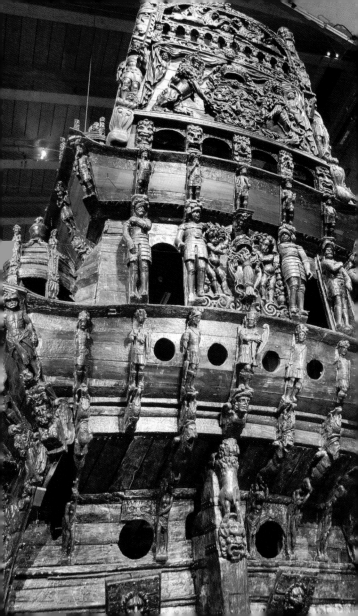

outgrown the urge – indulge it here amid models and actual ship interiors. Star of the show is the original cabin and sterncastle of the schooner *Amphion*, where Gustav III directed his attack on Russia during the 1788–1790 war. Models range from clipper ships to submarines and modern cargo vessels, and throughout the exhibits are navigational instruments, maritime weapons, figureheads, seamanship tools, and maritime art. Especially charming is the small exhibit 'Salty Memories', the sailors' treasures found in long forgotten seamen's chests: ostrich eggs, shark jaws, North American Indian arrowheads. A special section, designed for children under the age of 7 and open only weekends, recreates an archipelago land and seascape of boats and boat sheds where children can play. ⓐ Djurgårdsbrunnsvägen 24. ⓣ 08.519.54900, ⓦ www.sjohistoriska.se. ⓛ Tues–Fri 10.00–17.00. Admission free. ⓝ Bus 69.

Tekniska Museet (Museum of Technology)

Techies take heart! While the art mavens gaze enraptured at paintings, you can revel in what makes the real world tick. Play with the exhibits, do your own scientific experiments, converse with robots or just look at the examples of everything from an 1890s hang glider and World War I fighter planes to classic Volvos and Saabs. If it involves technology, it's here somewhere in this vast collection. An entire terrace is devoted to flight, from balloons to jet engines. Museivägen 7. ⓣ 08.450.5600. ⓦ www.tekniskamuseet.se ⓛ Open Mon–Tues, Thur–Fri 10.00–17.00, Wed 10.00–20.00, Sat–Sun 11.00–17.00. Admission charge, free Wed 17.00–20.00. ⓝ Bus 69.

Naturhistoriska Museet (Natural History Museum)

Out of town to the north, but still on the T-bana system, this is among the world's largest natural history museums. Exhibits are fun to tour, especially those on the prehistoric world and on space exploration. Ask at the desk for an English language brochure, to interpret the Swedish signs and labels. Hands-on exhibits explore outer space and the inner body. Cosmonova, Sweden's only IMAX movie, doubles as a state-of-the-art planetarium. ❸ Frescativägen 40. ❶ 08.519.55530. ⓦ www.nrm.se ❶ Open Tues, Wed, Fri 10.00–09.00, Thur 10.00–20.00, Sat–Sun 11.00–19.00. Free admission. ⓝ T-bana Frescata.

RETAIL THERAPY

Some of the city's hottest shopping streets are in Östermalm: Sturplan, Strandvagen and Birger Jarlsgatan. Modefreaks (a Swedish word, but it says it all in any language) will find nirvana here, at smart and trendy boutiques and designer shops. Names to look for in casual clothes are Anna Holtblad, Hennes & Mauritz and J. Lindberg. On the far edge seek out new names including Carin Rodebjer and Carin Wester. Pricey, but priceless. If international big brands are more your thing, look no farther than Birger Jarlsgatan, where you'll find Gucci, Versace, Mulberry and Hugo Boss stores. Or brave the better-than-thou salesclerks at ABCD for Dior, Fendi and Ferragamo. Just don't look for bargains in this part of town.

Sturegallerian A classy mall strictly for the well-heeled, with all the names the proper Östermalm local looks for, including J. Lindeberg and Face Stockholm. Here, too, is the spa-to-be-seen-in, the exclusive Sturebadet. ❸ Stureplan/Grev Turegatan 9. ❶ 08.611.4606.

Birger Jarlspassagen Beautifully detailed wood panelling and a

frosted glass ceiling frame the passageway lined with fine shops. Step inside for a sense of what shopping felt like a century ago, but be prepared for 21st-century shops inside, including J. Lindberg's flagship store and SVEA for fashions for the 15-25 set. ❷ Birger Jarlsgatan 9.

Sneakersnstuff Snub no more the lowly tennies and trainers; they've gone high class. Shop here for limited edition Nikes and Pumas, and for the brands in which the best feet are shod. A stop here could make you wonder if Swedes don't have a serious foot fetish. ❷ Asogatan 124, Birger Jarlspassagen. ☎ 08.667.5560.

Miss Sixty The name might mislead you: this is a shop for the young modefreak, not for the 60-ish. Keep up with the flavour of the week in clothes without paying a week's salary at this shop, more moderately priced than many of its neighbours. ❷ Birger Jarlsgatan 22. ☎ 08.54.505.152.

Östermalmshallen Caviar to pheasant, you'll find it in this beautiful food hall. Even if you're not hungry, stop in to feast your eyes on the baskets of orange chanterelles and deep red lingonberries. Lunch is available in any of the several cafés that open onto this lovely food-filled marketplace. ❷ Östermalmstorg.

Charlotta Kramer Choklad & Konfektyr Chocolates. Pure and far from simple, in lovely surroundings. ❷ Östermalmstorg 5. ☎ 08.601.121.

Modernity If it's art deco, modernism or the classics of Nordic design you seek, seek no further. This Scottish-owned shop has

◀ As the T-bana doesn't run to Djurgarden, there are other ways to reach it

collected the best examples of 20th-century furniture, art, ceramics and glassware. So if you want to take home a rare piece by Alvar Aalto, Arne Jacobsen or Poul Henningsen, stop here.
🅐 Sibyllegatan 6. ☎ 08.208.025.

Sibyllans Kaffe och Tehandel Since 1916 this aromatic emporium has blended the coffee served at the best addresses in Stockholm. Scandinavians consume more coffee per capita than people anywhere else on earth, and one whiff of this shop can explain why. Tea drinkers take heart, though, because the shop's other passion is fragrant and exotic tea blends. Try their own specialty, Sir William's.
🅐 Sibyllegatan 35. ☎ 08.662.0663. 🚍 Buses 62, 55, 41.

Alessi It isn't Swedish, but it's too cute to miss. Dress up your kitchen with some playful – but useful – accessories straight from Italy. 🅐 Humlegårdsgatan 20. ☎ 08.667.3550. 🌐 www.alessi-design.com 🕐 Mon–Fri 11.00–18.00, Sat 11.00–15.00.
🚍 T-bana Östermalmstorg; bus 1, 44, 55, 62.

Asplund Swedish designers are given pride of place in this show-room, where you'll find furniture, lighting fixtures, rugs and other embellishments for your own space. Look downstairs for bargains on last season's designs. 🅐 Sibyllegatan 31. ☎ 08.662.5284. 🕐 Open Mon–Fri 11.00–18.30, Sat 11.00–16.00. 🚍 T-bana Östermalmstorg; bus 1, 44, 55, 62.

Svenskt Tenn The decorator fabrics are the most famous, but anything you find at this haute-taste home furnishings design shop will be stunning, as well as stunningly expensive. It's the city's best address in home décor. 🅐 Strandvägen 5. ☎ 08 670 16 28.

Skansenbutiken For fine, but not overpriced Swedish crafts, you won't do better than at the museum shop at the entrance to Skansen (it's outside the gates, so there's no admission charge to shop here). Finely crafted woodenware in traditional and modern designs, knitwear, furry trolls, painted red Dala horses, dolls, hand-woven table linens, glassware, classic and classy interior decorations, jewellery, pottery and more are shown here. Inside Skansen, you can order custom mugs with your name or initials at the potter's shop (☎ 08.667.4023) or buy handblown glass at Glasbruket (☎ 08.662.8448).

In December, the park hosts a huge Christmas market, where you can find crafts of every type, as well as Swedish Christmas decorations in straw, wood, glass and gingerbread. ❸ Skansen, Djurgårdsslättan 49-51. ☎ 08.442.8000.

Ⓝ Buses 44, 47, tram 7, boat from Nybroplan or Slussen.

TAKING A BREAK

Chic cafés mark ultra-smart Östermalm, but you can still find a few modest places for lunch or a break from shopping. The museums of Djurgarden offer excellent cafés and espresso bars, as well as plenty of places to picnic in good weather. Skansen has several choices for lunch or a refreshment stop.

Dramatenterrassen Bask in the summer sun as you tuck into hearty Swedish specialties or sip a tall cool one from a frosted glass. The terrace is a rite of summer, part of Dramatens Restauranger, adjoining the Royal Dramatic Theatre. ❸ Nybrogatan 6.
☎ 08.665.6142. Ⓝ Buses 47, 69, 76 or tram 7 to Nybroplan.
Ⓝ Buses 46, 55, 62 Norrmalmstorg.

Fiore Close to the bridge to Djurgården, Fiore is a stylish place for a good lunch or for champagne brunch on weekends. ⓐ Strandvägen 56. ⓣ 08.528.09800. Ⓝ Buses 69, 44, 47.

Kaffe Bönan Sandwiches and quiches are inexpensive lunches at this popular café, or you can stop any time for a bagel or slice of cake or pie. ⓐ Humlegårdsgatan 9, Östermalm. ⓣ 08.662.4904l. Ⓝ T-bana Östermalmtorg.

Rosendals Tradgard The buffet lunch at this garden centre is a work of art, a flower-decked table covered with beautiful dishes of organic ingredients (many grown right here). The breads are served fresh from the oven. In the shop you can buy farm-made jams and artisanal cheeses. ⓐ Rosendalsterrassen 12, Djurgarden. ⓣ 08.545.81270. Ⓦ www.rosendalstradgard.com. Ⓛ Lunch daily 11.30–14.00. Ⓝ Bus 47, last stop.

Terrassen A popular gay-friendly spot for a snack or for just enjoying the view, this outdoor café is handy to the Djurgarden museums. ⓐ Sirishovsvägen 3, Djurgarden. ⓣ 08.662.6209. Ⓝ Bus 47 to Nordiska Museet.

Tvillingarnas Sjokrog Stop any time for coffee, or for a meal of home-style Western Swedish favourites. ⓐ Djurgardensbron. ⓣ 08.660.3714. Ⓛ Mar–Oct daily 08.00–01.00

AFTER DARK

Stockholm's trendiest bars are in the Sturegatan area, the street itself lined with cutting outer-edge bars and cafés where the glitterati hang out. Prices are what you'd expect in places where people go to be seen. Likewise, the restaurant scene is high-end, but it's hard to keep up with the darling of the moment. Be sure to get up-to-the-minute local advice if such things matter to you. For an early dinner after a long day at Djurgarden museums, you can find several places to eat right on the island.

Restaurants

Hotellet K–KK The darling of the neighbourhood yuppies and styleclones, Hotellet is still as good place to be and see – and to eat. The mix-match menu in The Grill offers grilled meats and seafood – veal, lamb, tunny, salmon, chicken or steak – sauced to order with green peppercorn, sherried braised onions, classic béarnaise, chilli hollandaise or other choices. The 45-foot bar is the local catwalk for hip designers. In the summer, stretch out on the back lawn with your drink. ❷ Linnégatan 18. ❶ 08.442.8900. Ⓦ www.hotellet.info. Ⓝ T-bana Östermalmstorg; Buses 1, 42, 44, 55, 56.

Sturehof K–KKK For all its size and popularity, this brasserie remains cheerful, friendly and a good value, with enough separate spaces and styles to make everyone happy. An outdoor café, bar and lounge satisfy various drinking crowds, while others head for the large dining room for excellent seafood, served until 01.00. If you're lucky, lingonberry-fudge pie will be on the dessert menu. Obaren is the late-night club, with a DJ and occasional live hip hop, soul and rock. ❷ Sturegallerian/Stureplan. ❶ 08.440.5730. Ⓦ www.sturehof.com . Ⓝ T-bana Östermalmstorg, Ⓝ Buses 1, 2, 55, 56.

Lisa på Udden KK Like its sister restaurant in Östermalm, Lisa på Udden specialises in fresh fish. Add the waterside setting, the view

and the excellent wine list to the moderate prices and it's easy to
see why a reservation is a good idea on a summer evening.
 Biskopsudden. 08.660.9475. Buses 44, 47.

Solliden KK–KKK Reserve a table for the traditional Smörgåsbord in
this hilltop restaurant in Skansen in high season, for excellent food
and views of the city. An a la carte menu includes many of the same
traditional dishes. If you can get a table, this is the place to be on
the Swedish National Day, for a view of the ceremonies and the
royal family, who arrive by carriage. Skansen, Djurgårdsslättan 49-
51. 08.566.37000. Buses 44, 47, tram 7, boat from Nybroplan or
Slussen.

Ulla Winbladh KKK This restaurant in an historic building does best
with the old traditional Swedish classics, such as meatballs or
venison with wild mushrooms. If you think this price range is a bit
steep for meatballs, you're probably right. You can dine outdoors in
the summer. Rosendalsvägen 8. 08.663.0571.
 www.ullawinbladh.se Buses 44, 47.

Vassa Eggen KKK The crowd is young, the food is good, the décor
chic and understated. Now that the what's-new crowd has moved
on, it's a place for those who care about the food, and enjoy creative
ways with venison, sweetbreads, squab and fresh fish.
 Birger Jarlsgatan 29. 08.216.169. www.vassaeggen.com
 T-bana Östermalmstorg, Buses 1, 2, 55.

Bars & clubs
Chiaro Dance to soul, funk and hip hop on the basement dance floor
– and until 05.00. Not bad, when you consider that the

atmosphere's friendly and there are more locals than tourists (unlike many neighbouring clubs). Upstairs is more run-of-the-mill. ⓐ Birger Jarlsgatan. ⓣ 08.678.0009. ⓝ T-bana Östermalmstorg; buses 1, 2, 55.

Sturecompagniet Très fashionable, très expensive and très hard to get in, the night club's five dance floors are filled with cool people sweating onto the very best designer labels. The décor is a draw, along with the chance (however slim) of spotting somebody important. ⓐ Sturegatan 4. ⓣ 08.611.7800. ⓦ www.sturecompagniet.se ⓝ T-bana Östermalmstorg; buses 1, 2, 55, 91.

Theatre & music
Kungliga Dramatiska Teatern (Royal Dramatic Theatre)
Swedish film legend Ingmar Bergman directed many of the performances in this art nouveau theatre. Its productions are mostly in Swedish, bus when foreign dramatic works are touring, they are staged here. It's worth attending a performance, even if you can't understand it, just to see the smashing interior at its glittering best. ⓐ Nybrogatan 2, ⓣ 08.667.0680. ⓦ www.dramaten.se ⓝ T-bana red line to Östermalmstorg, Birger Jarlsgatan exit; bus/tram 47, 69,76,7 Nybroplan stop; bus 46, 55 ,62 Norrmalmstorg stop.

Cirkus Built in 1892 to house the many touring circuses that visited Stockholm, the restored Cirkus lives on as a venue for musical performances, and is the favourite of big-name international acts (Bruce Springsteen played here). The restaurant is open in connection with the performance schedule. ⓐ Djurgardsslatten 43 ⓣ 08.587.98700, box office 08.660.102.071. ⓦ www.cirkus.se ⓝ Bus 47, tram 7.

Gamla Stan & Södermalm

Despite being neighbours, tiny Gamla Stan and sprawling Södermalm couldn't be farther apart. Gamla Stan is all that's left of Stockholm's old town, a warren of narrow winding medieval streets that escaped the wrecking ball of the 1960s tear-it-down craze. Södermalm – or simply Soder, as the locals call it – is brazenly and resolutely new and thrives on the razor-sharp edges of culture, fashion and lifestyle. Tourists crowd Gamla Stan's shop-lined streets, but few stray south of Slussen. These streets remain the province of the young, the hip and the in-the-know in search of nightlife. The thing the two neighbourhoods have in common is that each has a higher concentration of gay and gay-friendly cafés, bars and clubs than any other part of the city.

SIGHTS & ATTRACTIONS

Gamla Stan

Its buildings dating from as early as the 1200s, a tiny enclave in the heart of Gamla Stan is all that's left of medieval Stockholm. The island's place as the bastion of old tradition is further secured by the Royal Palace crowning its height, where the guard changes and the Royal bands march and play in appropriate pomp. These are streets and squares to stroll through, filled with character, lined by shops and galleries and scattered with attractions to visit. Expect to share them with throngs of tourists in the summer, since this is Stockholm's most picturesque island. At Köpmantorget you'll meet a determined-looking St George caught in the act of dragon slaying, and around Stortorget, a former market square, you'll see imposing old residences.

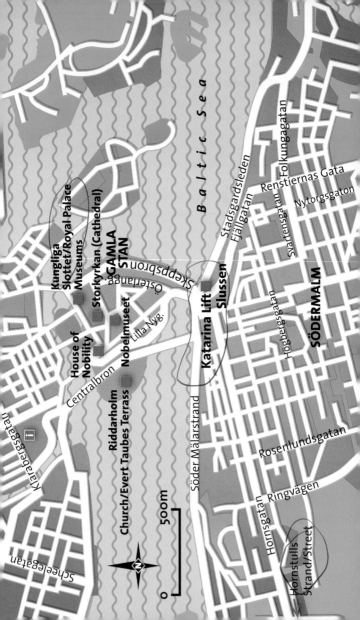

Kungliga Slottet (Royal Palace)

Fortresses and castles have perched on the hilltop of Gamla Stan since the 10th century, this one designed in 1697 and completed a half-century later. The Swedish Royal family lived there until the 1980s, when they decamped to Drottningholm, but their office are here and you might see them commuting to work any morning. The baroque residence has 600 rooms, and you can see some of them – the ornate reception rooms, the Hall of State with a silver throne, the rococo Bernadotte Apartments, the State Apartments (whose interiors are the oldest in the palace), and Apartments of the Orders of Chivalry. Various other rooms are included in the public tour on a rotating basis, with a different one opened each year. ⓐ Gamla Stan. ⓘ 08. 402.6130. ⓦ www.royalcourt.se ⓛ Sept–mid-May Tues–Sun 12.00–15.00, mid-May–Aug daily 10.00–16.00. Guided tours in

⬤ *On guard outside the Royal Palace*

English Wed, Fri–Sun 14.00. Note that Royal apartments may be closed due to state visits. Admission charge. Ⓝ T-bana Gamla Stan; bus 2, 3, 43, 55, 59, 76.

Changing of the Guard

Each day, in summer, three days a week in winter, the Royal Palace's guard changes to band music, sometimes with mounted guards. 🕐 Apr–Oct Wed, Sat 12.15, Sun 13.15. June–Aug Mon–Sat 12.15, Sun 13.15.

Storkyrkan (Cathedral)

The cathedral is Stockholm's oldest church, built as a parish church in the 1200s by Birger Jarl, the city's founder. Its greatest art treasure is the 500-year-old wood sculpture of St George and the Dragon, which experts consider the finest Late Gothic artwork in Northern Europe. Although it is believed to contain relics of St. George, its real significance to the Swedes is that it represents to them Sweden's defeat of its arch-enemy, Denmark, in 1657. 🄰 Trångsund 1. ⓘ 08.723.3009. Ⓝ T-bana Gamla Stan; bus 2, 3, 43, 55, 59, 76.

Riderholms Kyrkan (Riddarholm Church)

The 1270 Greyfriars Monastery is the city's second oldest church, and the royal burial place since medieval times. Its delicate pointed spire is a landmark on the city's distinctive skyline. The three royal chapels include that of the Bernadottes, the present ruling family, whose first king is buried in a gigantic marble tomb. 🕐 July–mid-Aug daily 10.00–17.00, mid-May–June, late Aug daily 10.00–16.00, Sept limited hours. Admission charge. Ⓝ T-bana Gamla Stan; bus 3, 53.

Evert Taubes Terrass

Beyond the Riddarholm Church, a broad terrace overlooks the wide channel of Riddarfjarden, with one of the best views of the City Hall rising above the water on the opposite shore. The ship moored at the end of the terrace is the yacht *Malardrottningen* now a hotel and restaurant (see page 38).

Ridarhuset

This beautiful assembly house for the Swedish nobles was built in the late 1600s, at a time when this part of Gamla Stan was filled with such elegant buildings. The gardens surrounding it are perfectly kept, as is the building, which is still the meeting place of the nobility. The meeting hall inside is decorated with more than 2,000 coats of arms of noble families. ③ Riddarhustorget 10. ① 08.723.3990. ⓦ www.riddarhuset.se ⓒ Mon–Fri 11.30–12.30. Admission charge. ⓝ T-bana Gamla Stan; bus 3, 53.

Katarinahissen

Although, like the other tower across town, it's a bit of an eyesore, the viewing platform more than 100 feet above Slussen does give a splendid view over Gamla Stan and the surrounding waters. The fare for the lift is less than a bus fare, or you can impress your friends by bounding up the stairs instead. It's not just for tourists – you'll meet Stockholm families there on weekends; it's particularly nice at sunset. ③ Slussen. ① 08.743.1395. ⓒ Mon–Sat 07.30–22.00, Sun 10.00–22. Admission charge. ⓝ T-bana Slussen; bus 2, 3, 43, 53, 55, 59.

Fjällgatan

High above the terminal for Viking Ferries, on Södermalm, Fjällgatan offers expansive views of the entire city. One side of the street is the edge of a precipitous drop, the other a row of historic wooden buildings with very good views from the windows. ⓝ Buses 3, 66, 53.

Street

The waterside promenade at the far end of Hornsgatan is the city's newest design neighbourhood, where a weekend market and an exhibition centre provide a gathering place for what's visually hip and new. But the 600-foot-long mosaic that colours the building fronts is reason enough for making the trip to the western end of the island. ⓐ Hornstulls Strand 1. Ⓝ T-bana Hornstull.

Gamla Stan and Södermalm Tours

To see the alleyways of Gamla Stan and explore some corners of Södermalm that you might never find on your own, you can take a three-hour walking tour, or separate two-hour tours of either. Rich in detail and the little stories that bring these neighborhoods to life, the tours are led by Stockholm Stories, ⓣ 06.708.850.528.

Walk through Gamla Stan with an English-speaking guide from City Sightseeing, visiting hidden courtyards and lanes. Each person in the group (of no more than 20) uses individual headphones, so everyone can hear. ⓣ 08.587.14020, Ⓦ www.citysightseeing.com. Departs Gustaf Adolfs Torg daily July–Aug 11.30 and 13.30.

CULTURE

Royal Palace Museums

The Skattkammaren (Treasury) houses the crown jewels – a glittering collection of crowns, orbs and royal regalia that includes King Gustav Vasa's state sword. The Tre Kronor Museum, in the cellars of the Royal Palace, shows the remains of the Tre Kronor castle, built in the 1200s and destroyed by fire in 1697, and relates its history. ⓐ Gamla Stan. ⓣ 08. 402.6130, Ⓦ www.royalcourt.se. Ⓛ Sept-mid-May Tues–Sun 12.00–15.00, mid-May–Aug daily

10.00–16.00. . Admission charge. T-bana Gamla Stan; bus 2, 3, 43, 55, 59, 76.

Kungliga Myntkabinettet (King's Coin Cabinet)

The most interesting of the palace's museums, this one is filled with antique coins. It displays coins dating as far back as ancient Greece, the world's first banknote and the world's largest coin, weighing 250 pounds. Labelling of these and the interactive displays on the history of money is in English and Swedish. Slottsbacken 6. 08.519.55304. daily 10.00–16.00. Admission free. T-bana Gamla Stan; bus 2, 3, 43, 55, 59, 76.

Nobel Museum

If you have a fascination for one of the world's highest honours, the Nobel Prize, or those who have won it, you will find this museum interesting. If not, you're unlikely to. The theatre shows short films about the laureates, and sound booths allow you to hear the acceptance speeches. Stortorget. 08.506.32200. Tues–Sun 11.00–17.00 (Tues until 20.00). Admission charge. T-bana Gamla Stan; bus 2, 3, 43, 55, 59, 76.

RETAIL THERAPY

Gamla Stan's streets are filled with tiny shops selling everything from the naf to the nifty. Österlånggatan is the centre for antique shops, especially those with maritime antiques. Vasterlanggatan is just as packed with small art galleries, handcrafts studios and co-ops, boutiques and souvenir shops completing the mix there. Tiny alleys radiate from it, with cafes, restaurants and more shops. Södermalm's shopping scene is quite different, of course. Here young designers have opened label boutiques, retro is in, anything over 35-max is out and alternative is the key word. Its main drag is Gotgatan, possibly the trendiest of all shopping streets in this trendy town. Giving it a run for the money is a burgeoning area called SoFo – south of Folkungagatan – alive with designer label shops, including Nakkna and Neu.

Kalikå If there are any children in your life, do them a favour and stop in here. You'll feel like Alice on mushrooms when you see the fully-stocked kitchen and hardware 'departments' with perfectly-crafted miniatures of adult tools and utensils. Clever finger puppets represent animals, storybook characters and mythological beasties, costumes promise to transform kids into Vikings or princesses. Prices are surprisingly reasonable for the high quality. There's another branch in Södermalm, on Ringvagen, next to the Clarion Hotel. ⓐ Österlånggatan 18. ⓣ 08.205.219, ⓦ www.kalika.se ⓛ Mon–Fri 10.00–18.00, Sat 10.00–16.00, Sun 12.00–16.00. ⓝ T-bana Gamla Stan; bus 2, 3, 43, 55, 59, 76.

Tomtar & Troll Tomtar are Swedish gnomes that – if well treated – will protect your home. In this shop they share the shelves with trolls, all of them handmade. ⓐ Österlånggatan 45. ⓣ 08.105.629, ⓦ www.tomtar-troll.com. ⓛ Mon–Fri 11.00–18.00, Sat 11.00–16.00; June–Aug, Dec also Sun 12.00–16.00. ⓝ T-bana Gamla Stan; bus 2, 3, 43, 55, 59, 76.

The Ice Gallery For the person who has everything, including a freezer to keep them in, take home a set of Swedish crystal glasses – ice crystal, that is. A set of 6 comes packed to stay solid for a day and a half, not something to buy at the beginning of the trip. ⓐ Österlånggatan 41. ⓛ Daily 12.00–17.00. ⓝ T-bana Gamla Stan; bus 2, 3, 43, 55, 59, 76.

Gamla Stans Hantverk Beautifully crafted work in paper, pottery, wood, leather and other media. Designs range from traditional to sleek Swedish modern, something for every taste.
ⓐ Vasterlanggatan 27. ⓣ 08.411.0149. Ⓝ T-bana Gamla Stan; bus 2, 3, 43, 55, 59, 76.

Scaramouche Long to be a medieval minstrel? A Viking maiden? A court jester? A Renaissance king? An Edwardian tart? Indulge your fantasy in authentic historic garb from this step-back-in-time costume shop. Fine replicas of ancient glassware and other historic repros, too. ⓐ Skomakargatan 24, near Stortorget. ⓣ 08.102.523, Ⓦ www.scaramouche.se. ⓛ Tues–Fri 12.00–18:00, Sat 11.00–16.00. Ⓝ T-bana Gamla Stan; bus 2, 3, 43, 55, 59, 76.

Ljunggrens Pappershandel A wonderland of paper, from delicate tissue-thin sheets to hefty hand-made card-weight fills neat rows of cubby-hole shelves and hangs from rods like newspapers in a Vienna café. ⓐ Köpmangatan 3. ⓣ 08.676.0383, Ⓦ www.ljunggrenspapper.com. ⓛ Tues–Fri 11.00–18.00, Sat 11.00–15.00. Closed Sat July–Aug. Ⓝ T-bana Gamla Stan; bus 2, 3, 43, 55, 59, 76.

Brunogallerian Near Slussen, this glass-surrounded mini-mall (the locals just call it Bruno) is packed with Swedish designers' shops, including Filippa K, We and Whyred. ⓐ Gotgatan 36. ⓣ 08.641.2751. Ⓝ T-bana Slussen.

Blas & Knada Contemporary designs in glass and ceramics in eclectic styles – and at high prices. ⓐ Hornsgatan 26. ⓣ 08.642.7767, Ⓦ www.blasknada.com. ⓛ Tues–Fri 11.00–18.00, Sat 11.00–16.00, Sun 12.00-16.00. Ⓝ T-bana Mariatorget; bus 3, 43, 55, 66.

Street Just getting started, Street is Stockholm's budding
Spitalfields, a lively mix of collectibles, vintage, retro and just old
stuff, with art, design and crafts. The waterside location is at the far
end of Hornsgatan. ❸ Hornstulls Strand 1.
🅦 www.streetinstockholm.se. 🕒 year round Sat–Sun 11.00–17.00,
closed Midsummer and New Year weekends. Ⓝ T-bana Hornstull.

OOS If it's young and hot, it's in this smart shop by four fashion
designers. Two new bright lights have teamed up with two well

⬇ *Explore the cobbled streets of Gamla Stan, lined with shops and cafés*

known ones to sell their own labels. Svartensgatan 12 (Mosebacketorg). ☎ 08.644.2970. Ⓝ T-bana Slussen.

Nakkna Begun by three fashion students, this label shop on the fringe of SoFo is a fave with stylistas who crave minimalist and monochrome. ⓐ Tjarhovsgatan 3. ☎ 08.615.2950. Ⓝ T-bana Medborgarplatsen.

Tjallamalla For clothes and accessories that are young and not what everyone else is wearing, Tjallamalla is the place. New young designers have a friend here in SoFo, where Liv Hoglund got her start. ⓐ Bondegatan 46. ☎ 08.640.7847. Ⓝ T-bana Medborgarplatsen.

Lisa Larsson Secondhand For yesterday's styles from every era, look no farther. You can join the Mod Squad or look as though you'd just stepped off the set of a Garbo flik. ⓐ Bondegatan 48. ☎ 08.643.6153.

Lovestore Got an itch to scratch? Anticipating a little action? Stock up here on fishnet stockings, exotic oils, adult toys and silk-n-satin anythings (or nearly-nothings). ⓐ Bondegatan 6. ☎ 08.641.7166, Ⓦ www.lovestore.nu. 🕒 Mon–Thur 11.00–18.00, Fri 11.00–19.00, Sat 11.00–16.00. Ⓝ T-bana Medborgarplatsen.

Neu Get these too-cool up-and-coming designers' labels, before they're hot, so you can say 'I wore them way back when...' No snooty sales staff, either. ⓐ Nytorgsgatan 36. ☎ 08.642.2004. Ⓝ T-bana Medborgarplatsen

Grandpa Grandpa may actually have worn or used some of the previously-owned clothes, decorator items or furnishings, but the

rest of it is brand new with a retro look. ⓐ Södermannagatan 21.
ⓘ 08.643.6080. ⓝ T-bana Medborgarplatsen.

TAKING A BREAK

With their heavy concentrations of shopping opportunities, both
Gamla Stan and Södermalm are fertile fields for cafes and daytime
watering holes. These are tucked into the narrow alleys of the old
town and sprawl onto the pavements of Gotgatan, Södermalm's
main drag, which is thick with cafes and coffee shops (Sosta, at no.
30 is one of Stockholm's best). Nytorget is all about cafés, and it's
also popular with picnickers munching take-away food.

Cafe Strömparterren Overlooking the water from the tiny island
that lies between Gamla Stan and Norrmalm, this cheerful café has
views of the Royal Palace. ⓐ Norrbro, Helgeandsholmen.
ⓘ 08.21.9545 . ⓝ T-bana Gamla Stan.

Café Kåkbrinken For the biggest scoops of the best ice cream, piled
into fresh-baked waffle cones, stop at this café at the corner of
Kåkbrinken, close to Stortorget. The frozen yoghurt is just as tasty.
ⓐ Västerlång. 4. ⓘ 08.411.6174. ⓝ T-bana Gamla Stan.

Wirströms There seems no end to the variety of beers on tap at this
friendly pub, a good place to mix and mingle, as well as to refresh.
ⓐ Stora Nygatan 13. ⓘ 08.641.4044. ⓝ T-bana Gamla Stan.

Eriks Gondolen The view from this lofty location above Slussen is
enough reason to head here to unwind after a shopping spree or a
tour of the palace, but the skill of their renowned mixologists has

reached celebrity status. ⓐ Stadsgården 6. ⓣ 08.641.7090.
ⓛ Mon–Fri 11.30–01.00, Sat 16.00–01.00. ⓝ T-bana Slussen.

Ljunggren Join the fashionistas for sushi and sashimi in this stylish
enclave inside Brunogallerian. ⓐ Gotgatan 36. ⓣ 08.640.7565.
ⓛ Mon–Thur 17.00–01.00, Fri–Sat 12.00–01.00. ⓝ T-bana Slussen.

Cocktail Deluxe If pink flamingos (the kind in a glass) are your
style, dress to match and step up to the bar at this retro-glam
drinkery. ⓐ Sodermannagatan 21. ⓣ 08.642.0741. ⓝ T-bana
Medborgarplatsen

Primo Ciao Ciao The pizzeria offers blankets to warm you on chilly
days at their al fresco café, or you can order take-away for a picnic in
Nytorget. The grilled veggie pizza with arrugola is scrumptious and
prices wallet friendly. ⓐ Bondegatan 44. ⓣ 08.640.0110. ⓝ T-bana
Medborgarplatsen

Loopen Marin Worth venturing to the ends of the earth (or at least
of the island) for Street – the weekend market – and for this
inexpensive marina at the water's edge. The hip, the restless and
young parents all join to watch the boats in a faux tropical setting.
ⓐ Hornstulls Strand 6. ⓣ 08.84.4285. ⓝ T-bana Hornstull.

Fåfängans Cafe For a peaceful place to watch the sunset over the
city, hop a bus to the Södermalm heights and have coffee at this
garden café. ⓐ Fjällgatan 37. ⓣ 08.640.5014. ⓝ Buses 3, 53, 66.

Hermans An all you-can-eat vegetarian buffet is served daily at very
reasonable prices. You can eat in the garden with a view over the city,

in a gay-friendly environment. ⓐ Fjällgatan 23. ① 08.643.9480.
ⓦ www.hermans.se. ① Daily 11.00–22.00. Ⓝ Buses 3, 53, 66.

AFTER DARK

For the hip scene after hours, head south, straight for Södermalm.
There's room for everyone, whatever your lifestyle, as long as you have
an open mind. Prices run the gamut, without ever approaching those
of Östermalm. The hippest is the area called SoFo, with Nytorget at its
centre. This is the heart of gay Stockholm, too, with plenty of choices
for both gays and lesbians. Gamla Stan is worth a stop for its cosy
bars (it, too, has several that are gay faves) and fine dining.

Restaurants

Pelikan K–KK Dining places don't get much more classic than this
large art nouveau hall with its tile floor, wood panelling and
Jugundstil painted ceiling, not to mention the Swedish comfort-
food menu and the schnapps and beer. It was popular long before
Södermalm was, and has survived long enough to be appreciated
again. Meatballs, of course, are a speciality, and so is herring, but you
can also get venison with artichoke or grilled wild duck; daily
specials are often bargains. ⓐ Blekingegatan 40. ① 08.556.09090,
ⓦ www.pelikan.se. Ⓝ Buses 3, 55, 59.

Folkhemmet KK A SoFo institution for reasonably priced food that
bridges the gap between Swedish home cooking and contemporary
international. The friendly buzz gets louder as the night wears on
and the drinkers in the bar (which has red velvet walls) spill out into
the restaurant. Book ahead on weekends. ⓐ Renstiernas Gata 30.
① 08.640.5595. ① Daily. Ⓝ Buses 2, 3, 53, 71.

Kvarnens Restauranger KK A funky beerhall where you can get good Swedish home-style meals or something a bit more continental. The bar in the rear, H2O, is a little more intimate than the always-crowded one in front. ⓐ Tjärhovsgatan 4. ☎ 08.643.0380. ⏱ Mon–Fri 11.00–03.00, Sat–Sun 17.00–03.00. H2O ⏱ Mon–Fri 17.00–03.00, Sat 19.00–03.00. Ⓝ T-bana Medborgarplatsen.

Roxy KK Contemporary Mediterranean-inspired dishes, using fresh local ingredients make this gay-friendly restaurant popular with a trendy clientele in the local design scene. Begin with a small dish, such as roasted tomato with chèvre cream, or go straight to the mains – perhaps almond-roasted saddle of venison with cep and Manchego potatoes and pear-chilli salsa. ⓐ Nytorget 6. ☎ 08.640.9655, Ⓦ www.roxysofo.se. ⏱ Tues–Sun 17.00–23.00, Wed–Thur 17.00–24.00, Fri–Sat 17.00–01.00. Ⓝ Buses 2, 3, 53, 71

Brännvin KK–KKK In good weather, outdoor tables overlook the Gamla shore, but in any weather, the atmosphere in this bright restaurant (once a customs house) is light and bright. Order the dishes à la carte or choose one of the combinations of three cold and three hot dishes for sampling of what Nordic cooking is all about: salmon, crayfish, venison, Janssons Temptation, fried Baltic herring, terrine of grouse, trout roe. Finish with warm cloudberries or an Akavits truffle. ⓐ Skeppsbrokajen, Tullhuset 2. ☎ 08.22.5755. Ⓝ Buses 2, 43,55,71, 76.

Ristorante Rodolfino KK–KKK Tuscan owners bring a little bit of Italy to the Baltic, in a romantic setting overlooking the water. Saltimboca, veal marsala or tournedos with Gorgonzola might seem ordinary enough in Tuscany, but here they are positively exotic.

You can depend on both the quality of the food and the warm ambience. ⓐ Stora Nygatan 1. ⓣ 08.411.8497. Ⓝ T-bana Gamla Stan.

Malardrottingen KKK A restaurant on a yacht is intriguing, even for water-bound Stockholm. But the Malardrottingen takes this far beyond the novelty value with good food, nice atmosphere and a superlative sunset view. Start dinner with salmon tartar and a zucchini timbale, or reindeer salad topped with fish roe, served in a basket made of crisp bread. End with either of the two local berries – a cloudberry pannacotta with *lakka* (cloudberry) liqueur or a mousse of lingonberries in a berry coulis. ⓐ Riddarholmshamnen Sodra. ⓣ 08.545.18790, ⓦ www.malardrottningen.se. ⓛ Mon–Sat 18.00–23.00. Ⓝ T-bana Gamla Stan.

Mistral KKK Book a table weeks ahead and be prepared to pay dearly for a memorable dining experience. Begin with only 18 people seated in the intimate dining room, add the presence of two very hands-on owners – the chef in the open kitchen and the maitre d' circulating among guests. Mix well with highest-quality fresh ingredients, stir in carefully-chosen wine pairings and the result is an evening of outstanding, if eccentric, food and good entertainment. If you're willing to splash out for one fine meal, spend it here. ⓐ Lilla Nygatan 21. ⓣ 08.10.1224. Ⓝ T-bana Gamla Stan.

Bars & clubs

Debaser Nightly bands play heavy rock, amplified enough to please the most hard-core of fans. This is Stockholm's heavy rock central, so expect lines. ⓐ Karl Johans Torg 1, Slussen. ⓣ 08.462.9860, ⓦ www.debaser.nu. ⓛ Mon–Sat 20.00–03.00. Ⓝ T-bana Slussen; buses 2, 3, 43, 53, 55, 76.

Mosebacke Etablissement Enjoy the view from the terrace in good weather at this combo bar, café, restaurant, disco and club. Check the schedule, since the music styles vary from jazz to pop to reggae to raw fusion. Saturday jazz brunches also feature live music. 🄰 Mosebacke Torg 3. 🅣 08.556.0 9890, 🅦 www.mosebacke.se. 🅛 Mon–Thur 17.00–01.00, Fri 17.00–02.00, Sat 11.00–02.00, Sun 11.00–24.00; dinner served daily 17.00–22.00, jazz brunch Sat 11.00–15.00.

Torget The atmosphere of this popular gay bar in the old town seems more like someone's living room. Meals (very good) are served, as well as drinks, to a wide range of music. 🄰 Malartorget 13. 🅣 08.20.5560. 🅦 www.torgetbaren.com. 🅛 Mon–Fri 16.00–01.00, Sat–Sun 13.00–01.00. 🅝 T-bana Gamla Stan.

Music

Folkoperan Unconventional and avante garde productions of well-known operas and new operatic works are the specialty of this opera house, whose intimate theatre makes the opera experience even more uncommon. Forget the stodgy image you had of opera – you might like this better. 🄰 Hornsgatan 72. 🅣 08.616.0750, 🅦 www.folkoperan.se. 🅝 T-bana Mariatorget, exit Torkel Knutssons gata; bus 4 to Hornsgatan/Rosenlundsgatan.

Stampen This Gamla Stan pub is Stockholm's first stop for serious jazz lovers, with top live jazz performance Mon–Sat and Sunday evening jam sessions. All moods of jazz are heard here – Dixie, trad, swing, rockabilly. 🄰 Stora Nygatan 5. 🅣 08.20.5794, 🅦 www.stampen.se. 🅝 T-bana Gamla Stan.

🄴 *Head out of the city to the archipelago islands or visit Gothenburg*

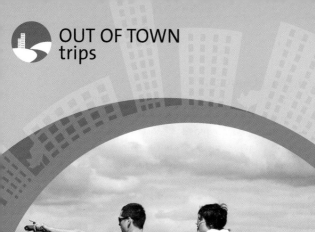

OUT OF TOWN
trips

The Archipelago

Less than half an hour from the heart of Stockholm is a watery wonderland of 24,000 islands, a scenic playground where city residents spend weekends and holidays. Some are little more than skerries, and others lie in clusters that form mini-archipelagos within. Those in the central archipelago are the closest to the city. A steady stream of ferries and historic boats connect these, making day trips or longer island-hopping adventures easy. Romantic lodging, camping, fine dining, local crafts, paddle sports, fishing, sailing, walking trails, historic sights, beaches and a variety of natural environments offer enough attractions to occupy several days – or even weeks. From June to mid-August, everything is open on the islands. In spring and autumn many places are still open, but only a few operate all winter, and the boat service is limited then.

SIGHTS & ATTRACTIONS

The scenery and the laid-back atmosphere of the islands themselves are the greatest attraction, each island with its own character. Some, such as Gustavsberg and Vaxholm, are connected to Stockholm by causeway or bridge. Boats to the others (and to Vaxholm) depart from Stromkajen and Strandvagen, in central Stockholm. At the Tourist Centre in Sweden House you can book excursions that include boat trips and activities, such as sailing or cycling and even meals and lodging, or you can buy an Island Hopper card good for 16 days of unlimited travel by boat throughout the archipelago.

Good information on the area is available from the Skargardsstiftelsen (Archipelago Foundation). ☎ 08.440.5600. ⓦ www.skargardsstiftelsen.se

Ferry & boat trips

A trip by boat to any of the islands is an enjoyable excursion, filled with changing scenery from the moment you board. Many visitors simply take these island ferries for a day on the water, enjoying the meals served on board as they watch the islands float past.

Three companies operate ferries to the islands. The Island Hopper pass is good for free passage on Waxholmsbolaget boats, with a modest charge of SEK20 on the other two lines. Full schedules for each line are shown on their respective websites or you can pick up printed schedules at their landing points. These are handy to carry with you if you are hopping among islands.

Waxholmsbolaget operates throughout the archipelago, with modern year-round ferries and historic boats. They board from Stromkajen, in front of the Grand Hotel. ☎ 08.679.5830. ⓦ www.waxholmsbolaget.se

Stromma Kanalbolaget ferries leave from Strandvagen and travel to the major islands and to Gustavsberg. Many of their excursions include lunch and /or dinner served on board. ☎ 08.587.14000. ⓦ www.strommakanalbolaget.com.

Cinderellabatarna boats leave from Strandvagen for the major islands. ☎ 08.587.14000. ⓦ www.cinderellabatarna.com.

◐ *The tranquil archipelago islands offer a contrast to the bustle of Stockholm*

THE ISLANDS

Gustavsberg

An island east of the city, Gustavsberg lies at the very beginning of the archipelago, accessible by bus or by ferry. The porcelain factories here date from 1825, but a brickworks was here as early as the 1600s. The harbour area has recently had a facelift, restoring some of the fine old buildings to make it a centre for design, crafts and fine glass and porcelain. The Porcelain Museum, galleries, crafts studios (70 working artists have studios here), factory outlets, and antiques market, along with cafés and restaurants are all a few steps from the boat landing (see page 129).

Within an easy walk are several other interesting sights. The Round House, designed by the architect Olof Thunstrom, was built as the municipal building in 1953, and Grindstugatan is the town's oldest street, where you can see artisans' cottages from the 1800s. Farsta Palace is a 16th-century manor house, now private residences. **Tourist Information** ❸ Turistbyra Odelbergs väg 11. ❶ 08.570.34567. Ⓦ www.gustavsbergshamn.se ⌚ Open Mon–Fri 10.00–17.00, Sat–Sun 11.00–16.00. Ⓝ Buses 424–440 (431–434 stop at Gustavberg Hamn) from Slussen.

Vaxholm

The easiest island to get to, Vaxholm is a one-hour bus ride from central Stockholm, and only a little longer by boat. This makes it the most crowded, of course, so if you hope to stay overnight or eat in a restaurant in the evening, be sure to book ahead. Luckily for those who do choose to stay over, most of the tourists are day-trippers.

It was King Gustav Vasa who first fortified the island, in the 16th century, as protection for Stockholm, building a fortress on a tiny rocky island. It turned the trick, protecting the sea approach to the city from both the Russians and the Danes. As Stockholm's gateway to the archipelago, Vaxholm became a shipping and fishing centre, providing fresh herring to Stockholm by boat. By the beginning of the 20th century, city residents had begun coming here to build summer retreats, eventually 'discovering' the entire archipelago.

The boat or bus arrives into the very centre of town, a broad quay where craftsmen and booksellers set up tables in the summer. The main street, Hamngatan, is lined with shops, cafés and galleries. A short distance and to the left on Rådhusgatan is the town hall and tourist office, facing Torget, a pleasant square where more craftsmen often congregate. Outside of town is a castle from the 1600s, Bogesunds Slott, which you can tour. ⊘ Bogesundslandet. ⓘ 07.343.43602. ⏱ Tours June–Aug Sat–Sun 14.00, July Wed–Sun 14.00. Admission charge.

Boats leave every 15 minutes (July 11.00–17.00, June, Aug 12.00–17.00) for Vaxholm Citadel, whose solid stone hulk guards the harbour. Inside the fortress is a museum (see page 130), a café and a B&B. For excursions in the archipelago, as well as fishing trips, SeaSafari is at the waterfront. ⊘ Strandgatan 5. ⓘ 08.541.75700. You can rent canoes and kayaks from Skärgårdens Kanotcenter. Engarn Resarö. ⓘ 08.541.37790.

From Vaxholm you can continue by boat to Grinda or to several other points in the central and northern archipelago.

Tourist information ⊘ Turistbyrån, Rådhuset. ⓘ 08.541.31480. ⓦ www.vaxholm.se (tourism page partly in English).

Grinda

Owned by the Archipelago Foundation, Grinda is just the right size to explore via the trails that criss-cross its piney hills or by kayak. A

paddle around the island reveals the variety of its shoreline scenery, from sandy beaches and coves to rocky cliffs. Kayaks are available at the dock at Grinda Wardshus. This *Jugundstil* summer home is now an inn with an excellent restaurant (see page 134). A flock of sheep live on the island's interior, which was once cleared for farming, and they take care of mowing the lawns. Along with Grinda Wardshus, the island has a hostel, cottages and a camping area for overnight stays. Because the island is a nature and recreation reserve, there is little commercial activity apart from two restaurants and a small food store for campers.

The two jetties, north and south, have year-round boat services to Stockholm, and the island is a good stopover on the way to Finnhamn, reached by a boat from the northern jetty.

Finnhamn

Finnish ships bound for Stockholm used to stop here, giving the island its name. Like Grinda, Finnhamn was once the summer estate of a wealthy Stockholm man, who built a summer villa here, and the island was later purchased by the City of Stockholm as a recreation area and to save it from over-development. It, too, is now in the hands of the Foundation. The villa has become a youth hostel (❶ 08.542.46212), where you can rent rowboats to explore the several smaller islands that cluster around Finnhamn.

Oak trees and rare wildflower species grow here, among outcrops of flat rocks that are characteristic of these glacially scoured islands. Stop to buy home-made preserves at the farm store at Idholmens Gard, an organic farm.

The boat trip from Stockholm takes about 2.5 hours and operates year round. Several boats arrive each day in summer, and at midday a Cinderellabatarna stops here on its way to Sandham.

● *Spectacular views are enjoyed along with a drink or meal on Grinda*

Moja Archipelago

Like Finnhamn, Moja is a whole mini archipelago of its own, and it has even less development. The village of Berg has a restaurant, a little homestead museum, a bakery, a few craftsmens' studios and the Dansbanan, a dance pavilion and social gathering point where they show occasional films. Stora Moja has a few shops and a restaurant and there is a sauna open to the public in Ostholmen. Apart from that the islands are the preserve of walkers, cyclists, fishermen and boaters, who enjoy its peaceful natural environments and seascapes. Trails wander through its forests and across its meadows. The main islands have very little swimming to offer. Bikes and kayaks are available for rent in the summer. The tourist office can arrange lodging in island cottages.

Waxholmsbolaget and Cindarellabatarna have scheduled ferry

service to Stora Moja from Stockholm daily in the summer; the trip is about three hours. Or you can take a bus from Slussen to Sollenkroka for a shorter ferry ride or to take a taxi boat ( 08.600.1000).

Tourist information @ Berg. ❶ 08.571.64053. ❸ Open mid-June–Aug daily 11.00–17.00.

Sandhamn

For the highlife – or at least the archipelago's hottest nightlife – and sandy beaches, follow the yachting set to this island at the outer edge, 48 km (30 miles) east of Stockholm. The Royal Swedish Yacht Club was established here a century ago, with its clubhouse in a 1752 customs house. The main village has been here since the 1600s, although the Russians saw to it that almost none of the original buildings remain. The close-set little red cottages that line the narrow lanes date from the 1800s. For a sense of the shipping that once stopped here, look for the old cemetery at the edge of town, where the stones show names of sailors from all over the world.

Restaurants and shops, tennis and even mini-golf and scuba diving offer diversion, and trails lead through the piney woodlands to a beach on the opposite called, curiously, Trouville. THE Trouville it's not, but a lovely beach it is, and less crowded than those nearer town.

The boat trip from Stockholm takes about 3 hours, or a shorter (and less expensive if you do not have an Island Hopper pass) option is to take the bus from Slussen to Stavnas for a one-hour boat ride as an interesting excursion through the narrow Stromma Canal. The 8-hour return trip includes a two-hour stop in Sandhamn, with a tour. Stromma Kanalbolaget . ❶ 08.587.14000. Ⓦ www.strommakanalbolaget.com

Tourist information ❶ 08.571.53000.

Namdo

Another little cluster of islands and islets with Namdo its largest, this is a place for those who love quiet and nature. Wild deer and elk inhabit the rolling western side of the island and the centre is covered in pine forests. Ostanviks, Sand and Solvik are the three ferry stops, and at the first of these is a working organic farm, Ostanviks Gard, and a nature trail. The farm also offers camping and a farm shop. ➋ Ostanviks. ➊ 08.571.56418.

In Sand, the small Hembygdsmuseet (Homestead Museum) shows island handwork and historic photos. ➊ 08.571.59047. ➌ July daily 12.00–15.00, early Aug Sat–Sun 12.00–15.00. A lookout tower crowns the highest point, Namdo Bote, at the northeast, which rises to 40 m (130 ft) elevation. You can hire bikes at Solvik to explore the island. Scheduled summer ferries from Stockholm require a change of boats in Saltsjobaden, or you can take the bus from Slussen to Stavsnas for a year-round ferry ride of about one hour.

Tourist Information ➋ Solvik ➊ 08.571.56017.

CULTURE

Several of the islands have interesting little homestead museums that recall life when they were primarily fishing communities. Apart from these, the only museums are in Gustavsberg and Vaxholm.

Gustavsberg Porcelain Museum

The astonishing collection of historic porcelain is beautifully displayed to demonstrate the development of styles and processes. It shows how closely design in fine tableware and decorative china mirrors the design styles of each era. Particularly interesting is a room showing kitchens of each era to put the tableware in its context. In the studio,

you can watch craftsmen create porcelain pieces and hand paint the designs. ❸ Odelbergs Vag 5B, Gustavsberg. ❶ 08.570.35658. ❹ May–Sept Mon–Fri 10.00–17.00, Sat–Sun 11.00–15.00, Oct–Apr Tues–Sun 11.00–16.00. Admission charge. ❽ Buses 424–440 (431–434 stop at Gustavberg Hamn) from Slussen.

Gallery Gula Byggningen

Inside the distinctive yellow building facing the harbour is a large exhibition hall that features brilliantly curated changing exhibitions of Swedish design and craft. Along with the Porcelain Museum, it forms the centrepiece of this smart new art and design district. ❸ Odelbergs Vag 9, Gustavsberg. ❶ 08.570.13211. ❹ Mon–Fri 10.00–17.00, Sat–Sun 11.00–16.00. ❽ Buses 424–440 (431–434 stop at Gustavberg Hamn) from Slussen.

Vaxholms Hembygdsmuseum (Homestead Museum)

The simple necessities of life on an island homestead are explored in this small museum of household furnishings and fishing equipment. Along with a café, the museum has a shop. ❸ Trädgårdsgatan 19. ❶ 08.541.31720. ❹ June–Aug Sat–Sun 12.00–16.00.

Vaxholms Fastnings Museum

Inside the impressive fortress in Vaxholm harbour is a museum showing the history of the citadel and the defense of Stockholm harbour. Scenes of military life are shown, with uniforms and armaments, and other exhibits focus on the archipelago's unique mining history. ❸ Vaxholm Citadel. ❶ 08.541.72157. ❹ June daily 12.00–16.00, July–Aug daily 11.00–17.00, early Sept Sat–Sun 11.00–17.00. Admission charge. Boats leave the Vaxholm landing every 15 minutes, July 11.00–17.00, June, Aug 12.00–17.00.

RETAIL THERAPY

The former porcelain works at Gustavsberg have become a centre for Swedish design, as well attracting a clutch of off-price outlets for brand names in porcelain and glassware. Throughout the islands you'll find small shops and galleries that display traditional island crafts and products. Smoked fish is a good souvenir of these islands.

Gallery Gula Byggningen In the same building (the original 1826 offices of Gustavsberg Porcelain) as the exhibition hall is a shop featuring works by outstanding contemporary artists and designers. Along with porcelain and ceramics are graphics and works in wool, paper, textiles, glass, wood and metal. Look here for the hottest and newest in cutting-edge design. ⊜ Odelbergs Vag 9, Gustavsberg. ❶ 08.570.13211. ⊕ Mon–Fri 10.00–17.00, Sat–Sun 11.00–16.00. ⦿ Buses 424–440 (431–434 stop at Gustavberg Hamn) from Slussen.

Gustavsbergs Fabriksbutik The factory outlet is a warehouse-like bonanza of porcelain, ceramics, glass, cookware and kitchen accessories. Nearby are outlets for Villeroy Boch and for glassware by Orrefors and Kosta Boda. ⊜ Tyra Lundgrensväg 23, Gustavsberg. ❶ 08.570.35655. ⊕ Mon–Fri 10.00–18.00, Sat 10.00–15.00, Sun 11.00–15.00. ⦿ Buses 424–440 from Slussen.

Antikhuset i Gustavsberg Specialising in the historic pieces of Gustavsberg porcelain, the antique shop has a large selection of porcelain animals, figurines, vases and reliefs by Lisa Larson. ⊜ Chamottevägen 13, Gustavsberg. ❶ 08.570.30577. ⓦ www.ahg.se ⊕ Open Wed–Fri 11.00–17.00, Sat 11.00–15.00. ⦿ Buses 424–440 (431–434 stop at Gustavberg Hamn) from Slussen.

Skärgårdssmak (Taste of the Archipelago) Carefully selected examples of the best crafts are gathered in a shop in the historic tower of the Factory Estate building, at the harbour.  Odelbergsvägen 11, Gustavsberg.  Buses 424–440 (431–434 stop at Gustavberg Hamn) from Slussen.

Galleri Lena Linderholm Bright, vivid bold designs splash colour all over this cheery shop. It's clear to see the influence of Lena's travels in Provence in her designs for ceramics, textiles and fine art prints.  Rådhusgatan 19.  08.541.32165.  June–mid-Oct Mon–Fri 11–17.00, Sat 11.00–16.00, Sun 12.00–16.00.

Glashyttan Waxholm The boutique shop shows art glass by artists of the calibre of Cecilia Nordkvist and Morgan Persson.  Torggatan 22, Vaxholm.  08.541.33456.  June–Aug most days 11.00–19.00.

Sommarbutik Handicrafts from the island are sold alongside groceries and locally-grown farm products and fresh-caught fish, in a one-stops shop for all things from the islands.  Finnhamn.  08.542.46207.  Open June–Aug daily 10.00–18.00.

TAKING A BREAK

Nearly every jetty where the ferries land has a café or snack shop of some sort. In the larger island communities you'll also find at least one bakery. Be sure to stop for sailor buns on Sandhamn.

Vaxholmsbagarna This bakery has a few tables on the pavement, a good stop right on the main street.  Hamngatan 6, Vaxholm.  08.541.31872.

Strömmingslådan Well past Torget, this garden-set café serves delicious herring, as well as other dishes that are good choices to takeaway for picnics. @ Trädgårdsgatan 12, Vaxholm. ❶ 08.541.30247.

Café Parkvillan Fresh-baked tea breads, fresh-made sandwiches and special attention to vegetarians make this another reason to visit Bogusunds castle. @ Vandrarhem, Vaxholm. ❶ 073.570.9271.

Bistro Framfickan Light meals, snacks and good pasta dishes are served here in an idyllic rock-bound cove. Take-away available for boaters and picnickers. @ North Jetty, Grinda. ❶ 08.542.49491. ❶ Open May–mid-June, mid-Aug–Sept Sat 11.00–18.00, Sun 11.00–16.00, mid-June –mid-Aug daily 11.00–21.00.

Sandhamns Bageri The famous sailor buns, an island speciality, are baked here daily. @ Sandhamn. ❶ 08.571.53015.

Sandhamn Glas A good stop for ice cream, coffee or a sandwich. @ Sandhamn. ❶ 08.571.53016.

AFTER DARK

While the islands, except for Sandham, are not known for their nightlife, they are known for a few excellent restaurants. Grinds Wardshus is primary among these, with a sophisticated menu based on locally grown ingredients. Most of the islands' chefs value the locally available ingredients, especially – fresh seafood from the archipelago. Desserts made with local lingnonberries, rhubarb and elderberries are especially good.

Finnhamn Café & Krog K–KKK The view from the big veranda is splendid, as is the hot-smoked salmon for which the restaurant is well-known. They will pack picnic baskets for you. ⓐ Finnham. ⓣ 08.542.46207. ⓛ Easter–Oct Fri–Sun, June–Aug daily 11.00–24.00.

Moja Krog K–KK Near the jetty in Berg, this small restaurant serves fresh fish from waters surrounding the archipelago. Smoked fish is an island speciality. Berg, Moja. ⓣ 08.571.64185. ⓛ mid-June–Aug.

Nämdö Hamnkrog KK This cosy restaurant close to the jetty serves traditional and continental dishes, with a sandwich menu at lunch. ⓐ Ångbåtsbrygga, Västerby 5, Solvik. ⓣ 08.571.56157. ⓛ May–Sept Fri 16.00–22.00, Sat 11.00–22, Sun 11.00–15.00.

Grinda Wardshus KK–KKK The chef gets seafood from local fishermen and cheeses and fresh berries and vegetables from archipelago farms, and his efforts have twice earned him the well-deserved title of best restaurant in the archipelago. Original dishes share the menu with creative takes on traditional local cuisine. ⓐ Grinda. ⓣ 08.542.49491. ⓦ www.grindawardshus.se ⓛ Jan–mid-June, mid-Sept–Dec Fri–Sun, mid-June–mid Aug daily. Bookings essential.

Sandhamns Värdshus KK–KKK Traditional old waterfront tavern that's been serving the public since 1672. If you're tired of fish, try the steak with red onions. ⓐ Sandhamn. ⓣ 08.571.53051. ⓛ Mon–Thur 12.00–14.30, 17.00–22.00. Fri 12.00–14.30, 17.00–22.30, Sat 12.00–14.30, Sun 12.00–21.00. Booking required weekends.

Waxholms Hotell KK–KKK Fine dining is offered in the upstairs dining room, while more casual fare is served on the outdoor terrace in summer. The smoked reindeer is excellent, but if you ask the chef's advice it will almost always be the fresh fish. Book ahead to be sure of a table. ⓐ Hamngatan 2, Vaxholm. ⓣ 08.541.30150. ⓛ Open daily June–Aug 12.00–22.30. Sept–May daily 12.00–21.00.

Dykarbaren Trendy nightspot and bar in the centre of town. Sandhamn. ⓣ 08.571.63654. ⓦ www.dykarbaren.

ACCOMMODATION

Grinda Wardshus KK This island retreat is a 45-minute ferry ride from Stockholm. The former country house from 1906–8, it is now a relaxing place to retreat to for a few days of hiking, bicycling or boating and kayaking around the island nature reserve. Rooms are comfortable and attractive. The dining room serves local dishes with international flair. ⓐ Södra bryggan, Grinda. ⓣ 08.542.49491. ⓕ 08.542.49497. ⓦ www.grindawardshus.se

Hotell Blä Blom KK Proximity to the harbour, the porcelain museum and some of Sweden's best outlet shopping, this is a chance to relax in an inexpensive family-run hotel, easily accessed by bus from Stockholm. ⓐ Gustavsberg Harbour. ⓣ 08.574.11260. ⓕ 08.570.31260.

Waxholms Hotell AB KK–KKK This pleasant and comfortable hotel sits right on the quay in a small town at the end of a peninsula. Accessible by bus from the city, it is still part of the archipelago and can also be reached by ferry from Stockholm or other islands. ⓐ Hamngatan 2, Waxhol., ⓣ 08.541.30150. ⓕ 08.541.313 76. ⓦ www.waxholmshotell.se

Gothenburg & the Gota Canal

The delightful little city of Gothenburg (Göteborg in Swedish) sits on Sweden's western coast, and is filled with attractions little known to foreign tourists. Boat trips on the historic Gota Canal begin from its harbour.

SIGHTS & ATTRACTIONS

The streets of Gothenburg's old town are a pleasant mix of architectural styles from the 17th to 21st centuries. A trading centre since Viking times, Gothenburg was home of the East India Company. **Tourist information** Göteborg Tourist Office ⓐ Kungsportsplatsen 2. ① 031.61.2500. ⓦ www.goteborg.com ⓛ May–Aug daily, Sept–Apr Mon–Sat. Göteborg Passes, which give free admission to most museums and attractions, public transport and deep discounts on tours and cruises, are sold here.

Maritima Centrum (Maritime Centre)

The world's largest museum of ships afloat, this remarkable collection includes the only surviving iron-clad monitor, as well as a destroyer, cargo vessel, submarine and light ship. ⓐ Packhuskajen, Gothenburg. ① 031.105.950. ⓦ www.goteborgsmaritimacentrum.com ⓛ May–Aug daily 10.00–18.00. Admission charge. ⓝ Trams 5, 10 to Lilla Bommen.

Trädgårdsföreningen

Gothenburg's Horticultural Society park is a beautiful – and colourful – oasis with a Palm House, Rosarium and glasshouse, as well as formal beds. ① 031.365.5858. ⓦ www.trädgårdsföreningen.se ⓛ Daily. ⓝ Trams 3, 4, 5, 10 to Kungsportsplatsen.

Masthugget Church
Commanding a hilltop, this striking church uses traditional Viking designs and techniques to create a distinctive Nordic art nouveau style. 🅐 Storbackegatan. 🕒 Mon–Fri.

Liseberg
More than an amusement park, Liseberg is Sweden's most visited attraction, with restaurants, a dance pavilion, live entertainment, music, shops and rides. 🅐 Gothenburg. 🕿 031.733.0407.
🆆 www.liseberg.se 🕒 late Apr–mid-Oct, mid Nov–Christmas Eve. Admission charge. 🚋 Trams 4,5,6,8, 13,14 to Korsvagen.

CULTURE

Konstmuseum (Art Museum)
Nowhere in Scandinavia is there a finer collection of works by the Nordic artists, including Carl Larsson, Anders Zorn and Edvard Munch. An entire gallery is devoted to their genius in capturing the qualities of Nordic light, and has works by Prince Eugen (see page 87). The Furstenberg Gallery shows early 20th-century Nordic works.
🅐 Gotaplatsen. 🕿 031.612.980. 🆆 www.konstmuseum.goteborg.se
🕒 Tues, Thur 11.00–18.00, Wed 11.00–21.00, Fri–Sun 11.00–17.00. Admission charge. 🚋 Buses 40, 45, 58 to Gotaplatsen.

Stadtmuseum (City Museum)
The 1760 East India Building was the headquarters of the company that made Gothenburg a European trade centre for tea, silk, porcelain and furniture from China and Asia. Now the city's historical museum, it displays Viking relics including the remains of a longboat. 🅐 Norra Hamngatan 12. 🕿 031.612.777. 🆆 www.stadsmuseum.goteborg.se

● May–Aug daily 10.00–17.00. Admission charge. Ⓝ Trams 1, 3, 4, 5, 6, 7, 9, 10, 11 to Brunnsparken.

RETAIL THERAPY

In the courtyard around Gotenburg's Kronhuset (Crown House) are craft studios and shops, while the charming Haga district is filled with antiques and speciality shops. And right in the city centre is Scandinavia's biggest shopping mall, Nordstan.

Helena Gibson Glashytta Brilliant colours and bold styles characterise Helena Gibson's glassware. ⓐ Kronhus Bodarna. ⓣ 031.711.8852. Ⓦ www.helenagibson,se ● Mon–Fri 10.00–17.00, Sat 10.00–14.00.

Göteborgs Choklad & Karamellfabrik The recipes for fine chocolates and caramels have been passed down through generations. ⓐ Kronhus Bodarna. ⓣ 031.775. 9064. Ⓦ www.goteborgschoklad.se.

Bebop Antiques with an attitude: this shop displays the works of Scandinavian designers from 1900 to the present in a gift-shop setting, not in jumble sale chaos. ⓐ Kaponjärgatan 4c. ⓣ 031.139.163. Ⓦ www.bebop.se ● Tues–Fri 15.00–18.00, Sat 12.00–16.00. Ⓝ Buses 80,85, 760, 764, 765, trams 3, 6, 9, 11.

TAKING A BREAK

Most of Gothenburg's museums have cafés, and among the shops of Haga Nygata are cafés with tables along the stone-paved street.

Café Kringlan The minute you step into this Haga café with the

● *The steps of the Konstmuseum provide a great viewpoint of the city*

pretzel sign, you know it's the right place from the aromas of their fresh-baked breads and cakes. ③ Haga Nygatan 13. ❶ 031.130.908. 🕒 Daily 08.00–21.00. Ⓝ Buses 80,85, 760, 764, 765, trams 3, 6, 9, 11.

Markets The Saluhallen, opposite Tradgardsforeningen Garden, has vendors selling breads, cheese and smoked fish for picnics, and little lunch stands where you can buy a tasty cheap bite. A short walk from Haga is the Feskekorka, a seafood market, where Kerstins Delikatesser sells delicious ready-made seafood salads. ③ Rosenlundsgaten. 🕒 Tues–Sat, Mon in summer. Ⓝ Trams 3, 6, 9, 11 to Järntorget.

AFTER DARK

Hamnkrogen KK–KKK You might not expect a restaurant at an amusement park to serve an outstanding meal, but here traditional

THE GOTA CANAL

The Gota canal, begun in 1607, connects a series of lakes to create a shipping route across the country to Stockholm. Leaving Gothenburg, the climb through the dramatic Trollhatte locks raises ships more than 100 feet. Learn about the canal's history at **Trollhatte Canal Museum**: start with the informative film (in English) and use the brochure that translates the museum's signs and labels. ❸ Trollhatte. ❶ 520.472.207. ❷ June–Aug daily 11.00–19.00, April–May, Sept Sat–Sun 12.00–17.00. Admission charge.

At **Sjotorp**, on the eastern shore of Lake Vanern (Europe's third largest), the Gota Canal proper begins. The last remaining hand-operated lock still in use is at **Tatorp**, and the oldest house and the oldest lock on the canal are at **Forsvik**, where a family of singers serenade passengers with folk songs and hymns.

Across smaller Lake Vattern is an amazing collection of historic and motorised vehicles. **Motala Motormuseum** ❸ Hamnen. ❶ 0141.588.88. ❿ www.motormuseum.se ❷ Jan–Apr, Oct–Dec Mon–Fri 08.00–16.00, Sat–Sun 11.00–17.00, May, Sept daily 10.00–18.00, June–Aug daily 10.00–20.00.

As you continue along the canal, across a meadow stands **Vreta Cloister**, the remains of a 12th-century abbey, Sweden's oldest. The impressive staircase of locks in nearby **Berg** is one of the most scenic spots on the canal.

Once an important city of the Hanseatic League, **Soderkoping** has preserved its medieval back streets, and the 13th-century brick church of St Laurentii.

Swedish dishes mix with trendier fare. Liseberg. 031.733.0300. Trams 4, 5, 6, 8, 13,14 to Korsvagen.

Palace KK–KKK Along with a café terrace on the park, the Palace has a magnificent bar, dining rooms and a nightclub. Dress smartly for this venue preferred by the over-30 crowd. Södra Hamngatan 2. 031.807.550. www.palace.se Mon–Sat. Trams 1, 3, 4, 5, 6, 7, 9, 10, 11 to Brunnsparken.

Fond KKK Chef/owner Stefan Karlsson is a one-man bandwagon promoting Swedish food culture as a living and dynamic force. He treasures local seasonal ingredients, and the dishes he creates blend Nordic and European traditions with modern culinary ideas and styles. Choose the sampler plate to taste several of the day's different main courses. Gotaplatsen. 031.812.580. www.fondrestaurang.com Buses 40, 45, 58.

ACCOMMODATION

Hotel Barken Viking K–KK The *Viking* is a four-masted barque, one of only ten remaining, built in 1906. An elegant hotel afloat, it is close to the Opera House. Gullbergskajen. 031.63.5800. 031.15.0058.

Elite Park Avenue Hotel KK–KKK This newly renovated hotel sits on the city's main street. Rooms are nicely decorated in contemporary modern style. Kungsportsavenyn 36–38. 031.727. 1000. 031.727.1010. www.elite.se/hotell/gothenburg/park

Sweden is synonymous with good design, even for the usually mundane

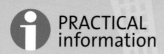

Directory

GETTING THERE

By air

As a major European city, Stockholm can be reached by direct daily flights from other major hubs.

From the UK and Europe SAS (Ⓦ www.scandinavian.net) offers the most options, with as many as six daily flights from Heathrow to Arlanda. Ryanair (Ⓦ www. ryanair.com) flies daily from Stansted to Nykoping Skavsta or Vasteras airports, often at ridiculously low fares. Finnair (Ⓦ www.finnair.com) flies twice daily on weekdays and once on weekends from Manchester, landing at Arlanda and British Airways (Ⓦ www.britishairways.com) has two or three daily flights direct to Arlanda from Heathrow.

Most flights from North America fly to Copenhagen, connecting with hourly shuttles to Stockholm. This transfer can be time-consuming because you must go through EU entry formalities in Copenhagen, then pass trough security points before boarding the second flight.

No direct flights are offered from Australia and New Zealand to Stockholm, so the best plan is to book the best price to a major European hub, with an onward connection.

Although there are fewer ready-made packages to Stockholm than to holiday-in-the-sun resorts, you can sometimes book air fare, lodging and car hire in a budget-friendly package. Ask when booking flights. Especially when booking such a package, it is wise to secure your trip with travel insurance. Most tour operators offer insurance, or you can protect your investment by insuring the trip independently.

By sea

Its location on the Baltic Sea makes boat a popular way to get there from other Scandinavian capitals and northern Europe. Most of these ferries also carry cars, so Sweden can be incorporated into a driving holiday, as well.

Denmark, Finland, Norway, Germany, Poland, Estonia and St. Petersburg are all connected to Sweden by ferry links, some direct and some through transfers. The two main shipping lines operating these are Viking line (☎ 08.4524.000. ⓦ www.vikingline.fi) and Silja line (☎ 08.222.140. ⓦ www.silja.fi) and DSDF Transport UK in Newcastle (☎ 01.912.936.209 in the UK). Swedish ports of entry

⬤ *Fleets of ferries link Stockholm with nearby islands, and much further afield*

include Gothenburg, Helsingborg, Malmo and Stockholm; ferries to Germany leave from Trelleborg. Buses and trains link these ports to Stockholm.

By train

The trip from London's Waterloo Station to Stockholm takes just over 18 hours, with changes in Brussels, Cologne, Hamburg and Copenhagen, and the trains boarding ferries for the water crossings. Other routes involve transfers from train to ferry for longer crossings.

Travellers from outside Europe who plan to use trains should investigate the various multi-day and multi-country train passes offered by Rail Europe (W www.raileurope.com). Eurail Selectpass includes rail travel in all four Scandinavian countries (or any combination of them) plus Germany, with even greater savings for two or more people travelling together. For travellers anywhere, Rail Europe offers a one-stop source of information, reservations and tickets. The monthly *Thomas Cook European Rail Timetable* has up-to-date schedules for European national and international rail services.

Thomas Cook European Rail Timetable ☎ (UK) 01733 416477; (USA) 1 800 322 3834, W www.thomascookpublishing.com

By bus

Next to a lucky hit for rock-bottom air fare, the cheapest way to Stockholm from the UK is by bus, about 35 hours from London's Victoria Coach Station via Eurolines UK (☎ 08.705.143.219. W www.gobycoach.com or www.eurolines.com).

By car

Automobile journeys to Sweden from the UK must include at least one segment by car ferry, which adds significantly to the cost. But this remains a budget-friendly option if several people are travelling together. Sweden, like the rest of the continent, drives on the right-hand side of the road.

ENTRY FORMALITIES

Citizens of Ireland, USA, UK, Canada, New Zealand, Australia, Singapore and Israel need only a valid passport to enter Sweden and do not require visas. Citizens of South Africa must have visas to enter. Visa forms can be obtained from the nearest Swedish Embassy or consulate.

EU citizens can bring goods for personal use when arriving from another EU country, but must observe the limits on tobacco (800 cigarettes) and spirits (10 litres over 22 per cent alcohol, 20 litres of wine). Limits for non-EU nationals are 200 cigarettes and one litre of spirits, two of wine. For specific questions consult www.tullverket.se. In either case you must be 18 or older to import tobacco products, and at least 20 to bring alcohol.

TRAVEL INSURANCE

However you book your city break, it is important to take out adequate personal travel insurance for the trip. For peace of mind the policy should give cover for medical expenses, loss, theft, repatriation, personal liability and cancellation expenses. If you are hiring a vehicle you should also check that you are appropriately insured, make sure that you take relevant insurance documents and your driving licence with you.

MONEY

Although Sweden is a member of the EU, it does not use the Euro. The local currency is the Swedish Krona (SEK), which is broken down into 100 öre. Notes are in denominations of SEK20, 50, 100, 500 and 1000; coins: SEK1 and 5, 10 and 50 öre.

Credit cards are widely accepted all over Sweden, and cashpoints (ATMs) are everywhere. The best means of obtaining local currency is by using a debit card issued by your bank that debits from your own account. Although many banks charge a fee for this, these are usually less than cash advances of credit cards, and are at a more favourable exchange rate than cash transactions or travellers cheques. The latter can be cashed at banks, post offices and in most hotels, as well as larger shops. Currency exchange services are in airports and near the central train station.

Banking hours are weekdays from 09.00 or 09.30 to 15.00 Monday through Friday; banks in central Stockholm often stay open until 17.00, and those in airports and other travellers' hubs may be open even longer hours. The post office at the central station, which also has currency exchange facilities, is open until 22.00 each week night and until 19.00 on weekends.

HEALTH, SAFETY & CRIME

While you need to be aware of your surroundings in any city, and avoid walking alone at night in doubtful neighbourhoods, Stockholm is not a dangerous city for travellerss and has a very low crime rate. That said, petty theft can be a problem anywhere, especially in crowded tourist attractions, so keep money safely out of sight and keep wallets and purses in a secure place. The Central station and Hötorget areas can be very crowded at night, making them a target for pickpockets.

Swedish drivers tend to be very careful, although they do take off from traffic signals at high speed and often travel very close to the kerbs in the city. So be careful before stepping off, even if the pedestrian light shows crossing safe, and stand back from the kerb while waiting at a crossing. Also, take great care crossing bicycle lanes, since cyclists seem to have the right of way over hapless pedestrians in these.

Medical care in Sweden is excellent, with modern clinics and hospitals. Emergency service is available to all visitors. Those from EU (and a few other countries in Europe) are treated free if they have brought an EHIC card. You must obtain this from a local post office before leaving home. Those without the card must pay for services, so non-EU residents should carry travellers health insurance if their own coverage does not include reimbursement, and should also consider emergency medical evacuation insurance, often offered as a package with the former.

TOILETS

Stockholm may have more public conveniences than any other city in Europe. Every museum and public building has one, and you can usually use these without paying admission to the museum (if you must pass an admission desk, just ask for the toalett). Public toilets are located in all transportation centres and in many other places throughout the city. If you want to be really prepared, copy the list of these, with addresses, from the city's website: www.stockholm-town.com, click FAQs. It goes without saying that these are spotless.

CHILDREN

From high chairs in restaurants and pram ramps on the underground to a storybook theme park in the middle of the city,

Stockholm loves children. Except in the snootiest of haute design venues, no one will frown at children in restaurants, where the staff will scurry to make them – and their parents – feel welcome with specially priced children's menus. Most museums have special programmes and exhibit areas for children, as well as lunch rooms where families are welcome to eat packed lunches.

Not only does the underground have pram ramps and lifts and buses straight-on entry without steps, but adults with children in prams or pushchairs (strollers) also ride free; children under 7 ride free anytime and those under 12 don't pay on weekends.

Here is a small selection of sights and activities in and around Stockholm that will appeal especially to children:

- The island of Djurgarden is packed with activities for children. Skansen (see page 89) is filled with things to please them, from colourful costumes, demonstrations and folk dancing to a zoo especially for children.
- At Junibacken (see page 86), children ride a train to meet the characters from the world of Astrid Lindgren's Pippi Longstocking stories, and can play in Pippi's house.
- At Aquaria Water Museum (page 90) they'll find fish and other marine life from all over the world, and the amusement park Gröna Lund is just next door. This clean, safe park has rides for all ages and summer concerts that draw performers from all over the world.
- Older children will be fascinated by the Vasa Ship and the exhibits in its museum (see page 89) and especially enjoy the chance to stand in a real 'crow's nest' suspended high above the exhibits.

- At Kulturhuset, The Culture House, in Norrmalm (page 58), are libraries, theatres, workshops and play areas for children, most of them free.
- Museums: the Museum of Natural History has an IMAX theatre and planetarium, and the Museum of Technology is filled with hands-on experiences (including robots).
- Parks and play areas scatter throughout the city, and boats are always appealing to kids.

COMMUNICATIONS

Mobile phones are in common use, and European, New Zealand and Australian mobiles can link to several GSM networks after changing the band to 900 or 1800 MHz. US and Canadian mobile phones do not work in Sweden unless they are specially equipped before leaving North America.

To call a Stockholm number from outside Sweden, dial your own international access number (011 in the US and Canada, 00 in the UK and Ireland) + 46 + 8 + number, dropping the initial 0 before the 8 . From inside Sweden dial 08 and the number. To make an international call, dial 00, then the country code (UK = 44, Ireland = 353, US and Canada = 1, Australia = 61, New Zealand = 64) and number, omitting the initial zero in UK numbers.

Post offices not only take your letters and postcards, but also double as banks, with currency exchange windows. The post office at the central station is open until 22.00 each week night and until 19.00 on weekends. Internet cafés are common and the Stockholm tourism website (ⓦ www.stockholmtown.com), has a list of the most current locations. Many hotels offer terminals in the lobby for guests, and a number have inroom connections for laptops.

ELECTRICITY

Current in Sweden is 22 volts AC, at 50 cycles. Australian, New Zealand, US, Canadian and some South African and UK appliances will need adapters to fit Swedish wall outlets. If you are travelling in other Scandinavian countries, note that outlets are not all the same. Laptops using only 110 volts will need transformers, as well as plug adapters.

TRAVELLERS WITH DISABILITIES

Stockholm has moved toward accessibility with more enthusiasm than many other cities, a process aided by the Swedish fascination with functional modern design. The underground T-bana system is quite handy for wheelchair users, with lifts and/or ramps (although some of the latter are quite steep) at most stations. Taxis are more difficult than public transport for those who use an electric wheelchair. SAMTRANS offers transfers to and from airports, train stations and terminals (☎ 08.522.500.00 weekdays)

Most hotels have fully accessible rooms and some have special facilities so that guests in wheelchairs can use swimming pools and other recreational facilities. DHR is the centre for information for visitors with physical challenges, and the English language section of their website although small, contains a wealth of useful information (☎ 08.685.8000. ⓦ www.dhr.se). Contact them for a list of accessible restaurants, public toilets and other information. Kultur- och Idrottsförvaltningen in Stockholm (☎ 08.508.26.000)

The Stockholm archipelago boats operated by Vaxholmsbolaget (☎ 08.679.5830. ⓦ www.waxholmsbolaget.se) are all accessible, with level landings, although the steamboats and several of the other excursion boats are not. At Värmdölandet, in the southeastern section of the archipelago near Gustavsberg, about 30 km from the city centre is Aspvik, a recreation area operated by DHR. They offer rooms and cottages, as well as activities and excursions; reach this by bus from Slussen (🕿 08.600.10.00; bookings: 🕿 08. 564.826.50. 🕿 08.28.28.34)

FURTHER INFORMATION

Stockholm

The new Stockholm Tourist Centre, located at Sverigehuset (Sweden House), offers information on the city and the rest of Sweden, with a well-informed staff ready to answer your questions. The entrance is from Kungsträdgården, but the address is Hamngatan 27 (🕿 08.508.285.08. Ⓦ www.stockholmtown.com; open Mon–Fri 09.00–19.00, Sat 10.00–17.00, Sun 10.00–16.00). Information about lodging, as well as a free hotel booking service, is offered by Hotellcentralen at the Centralstationen (🕿 08.508.285.08. 🖷 08.791.8666. Ⓦ www.stockholmtown.com/hotels).

Gothenburg

For information on Gothenburg contact the Gothenburg Tourist Office at Kungsportsplatsen 2 (🕿 031.61.2500. 🖷 031.61.2501. Ⓦ www.goteborg.com. For hotel reservations 🕿 031. 61. 2500)

Gota Canal

The main office for the canal boats is in Gothenburg, but you can see the boats when they are either there or in Stockholm, docked in either city centre (🕿 031.80.6315. 🖷 031.15.8311, US/Canada 🕿 212.319.1300 or 800.323.7436. Ⓦ www.gotacanal.se or www.coastalvoyage.com/gotacanal).

Useful phrases

Although English is widely spoken in Stockholm, these words and phrases may come in handy. See also the phrases for specific situations in other parts of the book.

English	Swedish	Approx. pronunciation
BASICS		
Yes	Ja	Yah
No	Nej	Nay
Please	Tack	Terk
Thank you	Tack	Terk
Hello	Hej	Hey
Goodbye	Adjö	Er-yer
Excuse me	Ursä kta mig	Ew-shehkter mey
Sorry	Förlåt	Ferlort
That's okay	Det är bra	Dee air bra
To	Till	Til
From	Från	Frorn
Do you speak English?	Talar du engelska?	Tahler doo ehng-ehl-sker?
Good morning	Godmorgon	Goo-moron
Good afternoon	Godmiddag	Goo-midder
Good evening	Godkväll	Goo-kvehl
Goodnight	Godnatt	Goo-nert
My name is ...	Jag heter ...	Yer heetehr ...

	DAYS & TIMES	
Monday	måndag	monder
Tuesday	tisdag	teesder
Wednesday	onsdag	oonsder
Thursday	torsdag	toorshder
Friday	fredag	freeder
Saturday	lördag	lurder
Sunday	söndag	surnder
Morning	Morgon	morron
Afternoon	Eftermiddag	ehftehrmidder
Night	Natt	Nert
Yesterday	Igår	iggorr
Today	Idag	iddah

English	Swedish	Approx. pronunciation
Tomorrow	I morgon	i-morron
What time is it?	Hur mycket är klockan?	Hewr mewkeh air klokkern?
It is ...	Hon är ...	Hun air ...
09.00	Klockan nio	Klokkern neeoo
Midday	Mitt på dagen	Mit por dahn
Midnight	Midnatt	Meednert

NUMBERS

One	Ett	Eht
Two	Två	Tvor
Three	Tre	Tree
Four	Fyra	Fewrah
Five	Fem	Fehm
Six	Sex	Sehx
Seven	Sju	Syew
Eight	Åtta	Otter
Nine	Nio	Neeoo
Ten	Tio	Teeoo
Twenty	Tjugo	Tyewgoo
Fifty	Femtio	Fehmtee
One hundred	Ett hundra	Eht hundrer
One thousand	Ett tusen	Eht tewsern

MONEY

I would like to change these traveller's cheques/this currency	Jag skulle vilja växla resecheckar/pengar	Yer skulleh vilyer vehxler reeseh-chehker/pehng-e
What is the exchange rate?	Vad är växelkursen?	Ver air vehx-ehl-koorshehn?
Credit card	Kreditkort	Krehdeetkoort

SIGNS & NOTICES

Airport	Flygplats
Smoking	Rökning
No smoking	Rökning Förbjudet
Toilets	Toaletter
Ladies/Gentlemen	Damer/Herrar
Open/Closed	Öppet/Stängt

Emergencies

EMERGENCY NUMBERS

Although no traveller plans on needing any of these emergency numbers, it's a comfort to know that they are handy in case you do.

Police, ambulance or fire ❶ 112

Main police station, Kungsholmsgatan 37. ❶ 08.401.0000.

Police sub-stations at Central Station, Sergels Torg, Bryggargatan 19 and Tulegatan 4

Emergency road service ❶ 020.91.0040.

MEDICAL EMERGENCIES

Should you become ill while travelling, you have several sources of information on English-speaking doctors. The consular office of your embassy, they can provide a list. You can also go prepared with the appropriate pages from the directory published by the International Association of Medical Assistance for Travellers (IAMAT), a non-profit organisation that provides information on health-related travel issues all over the world, as well as a list of English speaking doctors (Ⓦ www.iamat.org).

Emergency dentist ❸ Kungsgatan 24. ❶ 08.5455.1220.

Hospital ❸ Karolinska Sjukhuset. ❶ 08.5177.0000.

LOST & FOUND

Lost Property ❸ Klara Östra Kyrkogata 4. ❶ 08.600.1000.

Central Station lost and found ❶ 08.600.1000.

CONSULATES & EMBASSIES

Consulates, and the consular section of an embassy mission handle emergencies of travelling citizens. Your consulate or embassy should be the first place you turn if a passport is lost, after reporting it to the police. Consulates can also provide lists of English-speaking doctors and dentists and find you an English-speaking lawyer.

Australia Embassy ❸ Sergels Torg 12, 10386 Stockholm.
❶ 08.613.2900. Ⓦ www.sweden.embassy.gov.au

Canada Embassy ❸ Tegelbacken 4, 10323 Stockholm. ❶ 08.453.3000.
Ⓦ www.canadaemb.se

New Zealand Consulate-General ❸ Nybrogatan 34, 11439 Stockholm,
❶ 08.611.2625.

Republic of Ireland Embassy, ❸ Östermalmsgatan 97, 10055 Stockholm. ❶ 08.661.8005.

South Africa Embassy❸ Linnégatan 76, 10523 Stockholm.
❶ 08.243.950. Ⓦ www.southafricanemb.se

UK Embassy, ❸ Skarpögatan 6-8, 10593 Stockholm. ❶ 08.713.000.
Ⓦ www.britishembassy.se

US Embassy, ❸ Dag Hammarskjölds väg 31, 11289 Stockholm.
❶ 08.783.5300. Ⓦ www.usemb.se/consulate

EMERGENCY PHRASES

Help! Hjälp! *Yehlp!*

Call an ambulance/a doctor/the police!
Ring efter en ambulans/en doktor/polisen!
Ring ehf-tehr ehn amboolernss/ehn doktor/poleesehn!

Can you help me please?
Kan du hjälpa mig?
Kern doo yehlper mey?

The publishers would like to thank the following individuals and organisations for supplying their copyright photographs for this book. Stillman Rogers photography: all images except:
A1 Pix: pages 1, 5, 13, 21, 40 and 57.

Copy editor: Deborah Parker
Proofreader: Angela Chevalier-Watts

Send your thoughts to
books@thomascook.com

- **Found a great bar, club, shop or must-see sight that we don't feature?**

- **Like to tip us off about any information that needs a little updating?**

- **Want to tell us what you love about this handy little guidebook and more importantly how we can make it even handier?**

Then here's your chance to tell all! Send us ideas, discoveries and recommendations today and then look out for your valuable input in the next edition of this title. As an extra 'thank you' from Thomas Cook Publishing, you'll be automatically entered into our exciting monthly prize draw.

Email the above address (stating the title) or write to:
CitySpots Project Editor, Thomas Cook Publishing, PO Box 227, Unit 15/16, Coningsby Road, Peterborough PE3 8SB, UK.